Women
and
Choice

Women
and
Choice

A New Beginning

Mary Rosera Joyce

LifeCom
Box 1832
St. Cloud, MN   56302

Copyright © 1986 by Mary Rosera Joyce

ISBN 0-9615722-0-5

Library of Congress Number 85-081556

Manufactured by Apollo Books, 107 Lafayette St., Winona, MN 55987

PRINTED IN THE UNITED STATES OF AMERICA

Contents

Part Three: Finding a New Beginning

Preface

A long search into the meaning of woman began when I was a teenager interested in science, art, poetry, music, philosophy, and religion. "How can I develop these interests as a woman?" became the motivating question. It seemed quite clear that the female mind is different from the male mind. But simple knowing is not the same as knowing how and why. Discovering patterns and explanations takes time. This process of discovery has taken years of living, studying, pondering, and observing.

Since my journey began well before the contemporary women's movement in America, I was assessing the movement from its start, observing its course, and gradually seeing the need for a new beginning for women. Great good came from women's quest for liberation—more development of their abilities, and more effectiveness in shaping their society—but also tragedy and pathos.

In the old beginning, women felt a disturbing emptiness and a need to fill an inner void. But filling a vacuum is not the same as a growing fullness of being. We can put something into an emptiness, and we can discover later that it does not really satisfy the need. The void continues to make us uneasy. Finding an answer then requires another starting point.

Based on the receiving and integrating emphasis of the female mind, this book brings together many different, even opposing, viewpoints. There must be hope that women themselves, sharply divided by what are called liberal and conservative issues, can find a kind of harmony. By reaching beneath the surface of the conflict to something quieter and deeper, a point of convergence can be found.

We can hope, too, for man-woman friendship of the kind that does not move necessarily toward the bedroom. More inner freedom would give men and women the room they need to find a meeting of minds on the level of culture and civilization. Toward this purpose, lively discussion and debate over the message of this book among friends, in classrooms, in adult education programs, and in the communications media could encourage the needed awareness.

Women and Choice also brings together perspectives from psychology, sociology, history, theology, philosophy, and ethics. The subject—woman—has a uniquely global and integrating power.

I hope that the book will suggest and encourage a new beginning for many women, especially in the inner development of an affirming heart. As much as its viewpoint accents the woman's mind, it basically says that the heart completes the mind, and the mind completes the heart—a fulfillment we all desire.

Why, then, is this desire so often thwarted in our lives, and what are the impeding factors? How can we find our way around and through them? Many of us, women and men, can join in the search.

A Note of Thanks

The content of this project went through several versions. The final version, with the help of many readers, progressed through two rewritings. After that, the subject matter was expanded considerably, and rewritten.

I am grateful to Charlotte Martin and Fred Blonigen who read the first two writings of the final version, and gave close attention to structure and style. Charlotte, a theology student, put many hours into forming some of the sentences, arranging paragraphs, and commenting on ideas. Fred, a student of puritan literature, suggested some of the sources used.

James Hitchcock, professor of history at St. Louis University, read and commented on the earliest writing of the final version. Other readers who made valuable suggestions in forming the content in its earlier stages were Nancy Koster, Donna Steichen, John and Kathi Hamlon, Liz John, Nona Aguilar, Rev. Paul Zylla, Andy Hilger, Paul Piper, historian Dr. Stanley Idzerda, and Bible scholar Dr. C. Jack Eichhorst. Still other readers who made helpful comments were Jill Schleper, Mary Jane Brix, Nita Tabor, Carol Berg, Rita Marker, Flo Sullivan, Rosemary Borgert, Larry Simmons, Doug and Maureen Dahl, and David Mall. Thanks to Bethany Lane for helping me to decide how to begin.

My special, warmest gratitude goes to Kathy Schmit, Mary Kruchten, and Doris Theisen for their personal support and encouragement in this work. Thomas Hilgers, M.D., professor of obstetrics and gynecology at Creighton University, and Susan Hilgers provided encouragement by their enthusiastic appreciation of the views expressed in the chapter on a true sexual revolution.

Anna Terruwe, M.D., and Conrad W. Baars, M.D., were especially influential in my thinking about feelings and the emotional aspects of affirmation. Bob, my husband, shared intimately in the formation and clarification of meanings and values, and offered many valuable suggestions for improving the manuscript. Discussing ideas with him was always a cause for joy, an occasion for more insight, and a challenge to continue developing the work.

Acknowledgments

Acknowledgment is gratefully given to the following publishers for permission to use extended quotations: to Winston Press, 430 Oak Grove, Minneapolis, MN 55403 for quotations from Anne Wilson Schaef's *Women's Reality*, ©1981; to *The Washington Times*, Washington, D.C., for a quotation from Nancyjo Mann interviewed by staff writer and columnist Tom Diaz, ©August 3, 1983; to Arbor House, 235 E. 45th St., New York, NY 10017, for quotations from *Sex and the Brain*, by Jo Durden-Smith and Diane DeSimone, ©1983; and to John Knox Press, Atlanta, GA 30365, for quotations from Paul Tournier's *The Gift of Feeling*, ©1981.

PART ONE

FACING THE PROBLEM

CHAPTER ONE

HAVE WOMEN FOUND THEIR WAY?

Choice is the heart of the women's movement.

By expanding their choices beyond their traditional roles, women increased their opportunities. Many left what Betty Friedan, in 1964, called "the comfortable concentration camp" of housework, and moved into jobs, careers, and professions. They found their way into various offices of business and government. But have they found the answer to what Friedan called "the problem that has no name"?

In *The Feminine Mystique,* she told what housewives said when they tried to express their dissatisfaction. "Sometimes a woman would say 'I feel empty somehow...incomplete.' Or she would say, 'I feel as if I don't exist.'... 'I feel like crying without any reason'."[1]

Almost two decades after reaction to these disturbing voices started the contemporary women's movement in America, Anne Wilson Schaef, a psychotherapist, said she finds that women in counseling are still not satisfied. "We are beginning to discover our own capabilities, and we say things like, 'I want to make a contribution that people will remember.' 'I have no time for relationships. I must focus on myself and my work.' Some of us become more job-centered than men!"

Schaef continues, "Once we have 'made it,' however, we sit back and say, 'So what?' We look around and wonder, 'Is this

3

all there is? It looked so good from the outside, but now that I've 'made it' I'm bored!"[2]

"So what!" "Is this all there is?" "I'm bored." These more recent complaints sound strikingly similar to those expressed by women before the expansion of their options began.

Another writer, Megan Marshall, who interviewed women across the country, heard the same overtones of discontent. In her book, *The Cost of Loving,* she said that in every city she visited, women were sounding dissatisfied about their choices for achievement in careers at the expense of love, commitment, and nurturance, and for singlehood instead of marriage. She said, "I could only feel sorry that what had begun as a movement for liberation had in the end turned so many women against themselves."[3]

The nameless problem seems to be coming back again. Will it spread and get worse? Will Sigmund Freud's perplexity about women return to haunt us? He said, "The great question that has never been answered and which I have not been able to answer, despite my thirty years of research into the feminine soul, is, what does a woman want?"[4]

Have the new choice-minded women found the answer? Does an updated expansion in options and alternatives really satisfy the most persistent desire of a woman's inner self?

What Does a Woman Want?

Whatever else women desire, they basically want to *be* who they are. The same is true for men. But men are more inclined to look for themselves in what they *do*. They tend to be more performance-oriented. Because of this natural gender emphasis, many have thought that the male sex is dominant. They have assumed, falsely, that outward action is superior to inward being.[5]

Freud was one who thought that men are superior to women. In asking the question, "What does a woman want?" his

4

assumption about male dominance prevented him from finding an answer. He thought that women, because of their inferiority, envy men and want to *be* men. He called this condition "penis envy," believing, of course, that the penis is superior to the vagina and womb.

But women can bear children, something no man can do. "Womb envy" is just as likely in men as "penis envy" in women. Men in laboratories conceiving babies in dishes, and trying to build artificial wombs, could be suffering from an unconscious envy of women.

Both envies, however, are based on a negative view of women and men. Feeling inferior to, and wishing to be, the other sex shows a desire to escape one's own reality. This sickness of the soul does not reveal what women and men positively want.

While the new choice-minded women say they want the freedom to be themselves, they also want equality with men, and the ability to do what men do just as well as they do it. Women who want to be themselves, but who strive for equality by becoming like men, slip into a kind of envy of men and fail to meet the challenge of true equality.

The "problem that has no name" is rooted as much in a misinterpretation of equality (women becoming like men) as in a lack of equality (women regarded as inferior). In both cases, women cannot be who they really are. False equality produces as much frustration as supposed inferiority.

How are women interpreting equality? Their way of thinking can help to fulfill what they really want. Or it can frustrate them instead.

How Does a Woman Think?

A good way to test our thinking about equality is to see how we respond to words like feminine and masculine. Do we think that feminine qualities are just as important for life and civilization as masculine qualities? Do we really feel that they are equal?

Feminine qualities are tender and receptive. Masculine qualities are strong and productive. Is tenderness just as important as strength? Is receptivity equal in value with productivity? Is listening (receptive) just as valuable as speaking (productive)? Or is speaking more outwardly effective than listening, and therefore of greater value?

Though men can be tender and receptive, and women strong and productive, we spontaneously associate tender and receptive, or feminine, qualities with the female gender, and strong and productive, or masculine, qualities with the male gender. If we think, even subconsciously, that feminine traits are inferior, we will tend to think that women are inferior.

What, then, do we feel and think about tenderness versus strength? Are we really convinced that receiving is as important for life and civilization as working and producing and getting things done?

Our culture forms in us the feeling that achievement is more important than receptive stillness. Many Americans even find it difficult to observe one day of rest out of seven. And most who do so still think that the six days of work are more necessary and valuable than the day of rest.

Six days versus one—that is the quantity of the matter; what about the quality? Though we are not accustomed to seeing it this way, work and deep stillness are both important. Outward action and inward receptivity are equal in value.

Part of our problem with receptivity comes from our way of seeing it as passive and inert.

We all experience the difference between a receptive and a passive listener. We don't feel that a passive listener is really hearing what we say. We know that a responsive, truly receptive listener hears every word.

We also know the difference between someone who receives a gift with appreciation, and one who does not respond. Receiving is not passive and inert. It is active. It can be just as active as giving, though in a different way.

6

If we sincerely feel, and honestly think, that receiving is just as active as producing, though in a more interior way, we are ready to interpret gender equality. Otherwise our view of equality will be skewed. While a distorted view might seem right for awhile, it's frustrating consequences eventually become more than many women can bear.

Keepers of the Feminine

Well-balanced men have tender and receptive qualities. And well-balanced women have assertive and productive qualities. But receptive qualities in a man are feminine in a masculine sort of way, and are therefore differently nuanced than the same qualities in a woman. Masculine qualities in a woman are nuanced in a feminine way. If, for example, you the reader are a woman, you know that your feminine qualities would be more masculine if you were a man. If you are a man, you know that your masculine qualities would be more feminine if you were a woman.

Individual men are masculine in different ways and degrees. Each has a tender, receptive side that is unique to himself. If a man thinks he can be himself only by living in his Joe or Frank or Don masculinity, he represses (buries alive) the more receptive, feeling side of his unique self. He short-circuits his manhood.

To become well-balanced, a man does not have to get himself into a balancing act between masculine and feminine traits. He needs only to accept the more receptive side of his own masculine self—whatever degree or kind of receptivity that might be.

Both women and men can be keepers, or protectors, of the receptive side of human life and civilization. But men are not as inclined that way. When men over-emphasize masculine qualities, women should be quick to seek a balance.

When a work-ethic or a production-mentality begins to take over a nation's culture, women should become immediate critics of this masculine excess. Men are not as likely to notice such extremes. They can get along without the receptive side of themselves more easily than women can.

A work-ethic and a production-mentality formed our culture from its very beginning. Men always dominated the public sphere of life, thus giving our civilization a heavily masculine character.

When the Industrial Revolution separated many kinds of work from the home, the division between the public and private domains widened to a chasm. Women were confined to private or domestic life, while men went out to factories and other public institutions.

Thus women exercised little balancing influence in the public domain. The masculine attitude of *control over* nature dominated the entire character of the culture. The more feminine attitude of sensitive cooperation with nature, regarded as weak and inferior, receded from awareness and almost disappeared.

Where, now, are the keepers of the feminine? They are meant to care for the feminine side of life in the public, as well as in the private, domain. Both domestic and civil affairs need the balance of feminine and masculine characteristics.

But how can women have a balancing effect if they do not understand the feminine side of themselves, especially the feminine side of their minds? How can they promote the urgently needed wholeness of their culture if they do not understand the masculine side of themselves in its relation to the feminine? If women misinterpret themselves, they cannot know how to move into the public domain as whole, balanced persons bringing the gift of a feminine emphasis. All the "how to" manuals available cannot help them if they are mistaken about who they are as women.

The Key

The key to a woman's concept of female wholeness and gender equality is found in her way of relating with the masculine side of herself. She can do this in four possible ways, only one of which can lead her to the wholeness and equality she desires.

1. She can identify herself rather exclusively with her feminine qualities, then look for an all-male, half-man to balance and complete her. She can let *him* be her masculinity for her. Romanticism and domestic confinement are based on this extreme feminization of women.
2. She can identify with men by trying to do things in a man's way, or by "becoming a man."
3. She can reduce herself and everyone else to a kind of sexlessness (which many call androgyny), in which all persons are thought to be masculine and feminine without any particular gender emphasis.
4. She can develop the masculine side of herself in her own way, both truly feminine and uniquely individual.

Is a woman identical with the feminine side of herself? Is she identical with the masculine side? Is she identical with everyone else viewed as equally masculine and feminine without a gender emphasis? These three ways of thinking about herself lead a woman to ultimate discontent, to "the problem that has no name," and eventually to complaints of emptiness, incompleteness, and boredom.

A woman does not have to find completion by letting a man become her masculinity for her. Neither does she have to prove her equality with men by identifying with their masculine ways. Nor does she have to become equal by making everyone masculine and feminine in the same way without a whole-person gender emphasis. She really needs to develop her female self in a feminine way so she can develop her masculinity in a feminine way. Then her masculine qualities will not dominate her

9

femaleness, but will enhance, deepen, and strengthen it instead. This is the only way that a woman can begin to answer Freud's question by saying, "I want to *be* myself," really knowing ho· and why.

A woman who "becomes a man," though she is liberated from the romantic style of male domination, simply moves into another style of the same male dominance. Though she might call this move into masculinity her liberation, the masculine side of herself controls the feminine side just as completely as any man ever controlled a woman. True liberation happens only when a woman develops the masculine side of herself in her own feminine way.

The starkly crucial question is, *how* are women supposed to find their own way in a civilization that is almost entirely formed by a masculine mentality? How, especially, can they find their own minds when the mentality in the very air they breathe is thoroughly masculine?

The answer is to see clearly this masculine character of civilization, to refuse to become masculinized by it, to find the feminine side of civilization, and to bring the feminine and masculine sides together in balance and wholeness.

Have women found this answer? Have they seen that the keepers of the feminine are called to assert the equal importance of the feminine with the masculine, as well as the unity of the two? Have they realized that the power for feminine-masculine integration is precisely the feminine power of receptivity? Do they know that unity is received, not produced, because it is already there in a hidden, or buried, way?

The Feminine Mistake

Women have not found the answer. What they have found, however, has seemed to them the logical thing to do.

When machines and appliances began to reduce the drudgery of their domestic chores, many women started to sense a strange emptiness in their lives. Besides feeling inferior and unappreciated for what they were doing at home, they felt an increasing need to liberate their power of choice, to develop the masculine side of themselves, and to take part in the public processes of civilization. Husband, children, and home no longer seemed to be enough for them. So they began to move, in ever increasing numbers, into public life.

But most of these women failed to see the powerful, almost totally masculine character of the public domain. Lacking this necessary insight, they stepped boldly into the trap. They developed their minds and their skills in male ways, and they insisted they could do this just the same as, and just as well as, men.

While women were busy trying to prove their equality in jobs and careers, "the problem that has no name" was forced underground. The public realm of work buried "the problem" as effectively, for a time, as the private realm of housework had done.

But the emptiness could not be filled with careers any more than it could be filled with housework. What women really wanted—the freedom to be themselves in true equality with men—was as unsatisfied in the feminine mistake as in "the feminine mystique." What women really wanted was as frustrated in the masculine trap of public productivity as in "the comfortable concentration camp" (the feminine trap) of housework.

Many women do not know this yet. They do not realize that "the problem" *is* coming back again; that the answer they were seeking is not yet found.

CHAPTER TWO

STEPPING INTO THE MASCULINE TRAP

Freedom to function as well as men in the world of jobs, careers, and professions depends, for a great number of American women, on what they call "reproductive freedom." Whether and when to bear a child seems to them the crucial choice that makes most other choices possible. They also regard total freedom of choice about childbearing as the key to their liberation from male control.

But we need to wonder whether the prevailing male system would allow women to "control their own bodies" if this permission would not serve the self-interests of men. What looks exclusively like a woman's right to choose could also be a male maneuver to obtain a greater advantage for men. And, in order to secure this advantage, the male mind could be controlling the female mind while encouraging the idea that women are controlling their own minds.

If such is the case, most men would not be fully aware of what is happening. Many would not approve. But a masculine mentality of a particular kind—one that is partly or largely subconscious—could be pursuing its female-controlling purposes, even in men who think they are promoting the independence of women. At the same time, this mentality could be assuring women, and men too, that American women are now the sole origin of their own way of thinking and choosing.

New, updated women are clever and assertive about their own autonomy. But are they also wise?

Are Women Controlling Their Own Bodies?

Many women insist that they can be equal with men only if they have easy access to contraceptives, tubal ligation, and abortion. Most, if not all, of the tools and techniques for these procedures were invented by men. Most of the time men insert the IUDs, prescribe the chemicals, and perform the tubal ligations and abortions. Most of the time men receive the money women pay as they try to control their bodies in these ways. The servicing males actively promote the idea that women's bodies, in their natural state, are, indeed, out of control. So they invent all sorts of strategies and contrivances to remedy the disorder, apply them, and collect the fee.

Even when the physicians are women, they function harmoniously in a profession that is almost totally formed by an extreme masculine mentality. This mentality is geared toward controlling nature rather than oriented toward cooperating with nature.

The use of drugs and surgery does not necessarily require, but is most often adopted by, an imposing attitude of control that attacks problems head on. More indirect and natural methods of health care such as nutritional counseling, relaxation therapy, and natural family planning, whether practiced by women or men, are more holistic and feminine-masculine in character.

Nevertheless, excessively masculine approaches to the body-control of women are professionally adopted and socially accepted. The more balanced approaches, with their basically feminine receptivity toward nature, are widely ignored and regarded as inferior.

If we can allow ourselves to be objective, we can see that modern medicine is treating the female generative system as if it were defective by nature, and so far inferior to that of the male that she needs his technology to correct and improve her body. We can see women falling into lock step with society's professional controllers of disease. We can hear women say by their attitude and behavior, if not by their words, "My unmedicated, surgically uncorrected body is my enemy. It is an obstacle to my freedom. It keeps me under male domination."

Some great thinkers of the Western world described women as defects of nature. If these men could see the pills, injections, chemicals and surgeries that millions of supposedly healthy women find absolutely necessary today, they might be hardened in their views. They might think the modern female uses these sex-related medications, appliances, and surgeries, and needs so much male medical expertise, because she is naturally defective and her body is naturally out of control.

Are women's bodies basically out of control, and therefore in critical need of management by the various imposing methods now in use? Are the normal processes of women's bodies diseased? Do women really accept the persistent male bias that sees their bodies as defective and inferior, and as therefore needing scientifically applied controls?

A woman regulates her own body, in her own way as a woman, only when she sees its natural functions as healthy rather than defective, and when she cooperates with these functions. This holistic approach of cooperation with nature (holistic because it includes feminine sensitivities along with masculine ingenuity) involves her knowledge and appreciation of her body. She knows and appreciates her fertility as part of her personhood.

But if a woman does not believe herself capable of understanding her body and its functions, she tends to regard her fertility as a dark, mysterious threat to her freedom. She is then likely to choose ignorance of her fertility cycles rather than knowledge. And she is likely, also, to control the perceived threat of her body by applying overly masculine techniques to its processes. Unwittingly, she thereby endorses the supposed

14

inferiority of the feminine, and domination by the masculine, no matter how much she otherwise champions their equality.

But her hopelessness about her mental capacity and bodily integrity is not warranted. Natural methods of fertility regulation (without contraceptives) are now highly developed and quite easily learned by motivated people These more feminine techniques require a woman's appreciation not only of her body but also of her mind.[1]

No insinuations of feminine inferiority are built into methods of natural family planning. Yet most women are still choosing overly masculine approaches to body control. And they are still choosing the lack of self-knowledge these methods permit.

This *coupling of choice with unawareness* is vividly portrayed by Nancyjo Mann, founder of Women Exploited by Abortion. In her statement to *The Washington Times,* she told about her abortion and the lack of knowledge involved in her choice.

> I went in and asked, "What are you going to do to me?" All he did was look at my stomach and say, "I'm going to take a little fluid out, put a little fluid in, you'll have severe cramps, and expel the fetus."
>
> I said, "Is that all?" He said, "That's all."
>
> It did not sound too bad. But what that doctor described to me was not the truth....
>
> Once they put in the saline, there's no way to reverse it. And for the next hour and a half I felt my daughter thrash around violently while she was being choked, poisoned, burned and suffocated to death. *I didn't know* (emphasis added) any of that was going to happen. And I remember talking to her and I remember telling her I didn't want to do this, I wished she could live. And yet she was dying and I remember her very last kick on her left side. She had no strength left.
>
> I've tried to imagine that kind of death, a pillow put over us, suffocating. In four minutes we'd pass out.

We'd have that gift of passing out and then dying. But it took her an hour and a half just to die.

Then I was given an intravenous injection to help stimulate labor and I went into hard labor for 12 hours. And at 5:30 AM on the 31st of October I delivered my daughter whose name is now Charmaine Marie. She was 14 inches long. She weighed over a pound and a half. She had a head of hair and her eyes were opening.

I got to hold her because the nurses didn't make it to the room on time. I delivered my girl myself. They grabbed her out of my hands and threw her, threw her, into a bedpan.[2]

Why did the abortionist deny Nancyjo Mann so much information? Did he believe that women make their best choices in the dark? Did he place any value on the woman's right to know the facts? What value did he place, instead, on her cash? How many women would go through with an abortion if they were fully informed about the life they are carrying, about what is involved in the abortion itself, and about the physical and psychological consequences to themselves?

Even the United States Supreme Court has ruled as though women have the right to choose without the knowledge that would make their choice informed. In June of 1983, the Court nullified an Akron, Ohio ordinance that required physicians to inform women about the dangers of, and alternatives to, abortion, and also about the stage of development of the prenatal child. Six of the male Justices declared unconstitutional this reasonable requirement for an informed choice. Sandra Day O'Connor, the only woman on the Court, and two of the male Justices, dissented.

The effect of the majority's decision was to keep women in the dark ages while they made choices about "controlling their bodies." *The idea seemed to be that the less a woman knows, the more free her choice will be.* Ironically, many women are willing, even determined, not to claim their right to know.

16

In the environment of this protected ignorance, one young female said, "We were lied to and deliberately misinformed. A case worker said that all I was carrying was a tiny blob of tissue." Another said, "I realized my mistake too late, as I watched a glass container filling with what I knew was the remains of my baby's body. Afterward I had frequent nightmares and suffered deep depression. When I sought professional help, I was coldly treated and was told there was no such thing as abortion trauma."

Dr. Eloise Jones, a Toronto psychiatrist, explained why abortion trauma caused her to stop making abortion referrals. "An abortion has not helped the self-image of any woman I have talked with. I was listening to one recently, who, shortly after an abortion, claimed that it had not affected her and that it was a perfectly justified action. However, I later discovered that she was very frightened lest her teenage daughter discover what she had done, and since the abortion, she has become increasingly tearful, hostile and unresponsive to her husband. In her and in others, I have been presented with psychosomatic illness, sexual frigidity, hatred for a boyfriend or spouse, anxiety, all kinds of neurotic disturbances and some deep depressive reactions....We are beginning to see the problems of women who had abortions three or four years ago surfacing."[3]

Women who seek professional counseling rarely mention abortion as their presenting complaint. According to Terry Selby (Counseling Associates, Bemidji, Minnesota), a past abortion, in the course of treatment, often shows up as a cause of a woman's problems. Depression, anorexia, suicide attempts, drug abuse, alcoholism, family conflicts, and other disturbances appear on the surface. Beneath the symptoms, however, a past, and sometimes even a forgotten, abortion is often a (the) hidden cause.

Selby says, "The denial continues after the abortion, and is manifest in the woman's unwillingness to talk about it, in her complete repression of her emotions relative to the abortion, and in her selective repression of her memory of the procedure."

17

A large part of the problem is that women are not informed about the psychological complications of legal abortion.[4] Nor are they told about the many documented physical complications.[5] Often they do not know that women who have abortions suffer, in subsequent pregnancies, more fetal deaths, more premature births, and more delivery complications than those who never had abortions. They do not realize that the feminine side of their female nature is deeply violated by abortion, while the masculine side might seem, at first, to go unscathed.

A woman who can undergo an abortion without any apparent psychic damage might be able to turn off her conscious mind with sophisticated slogans about freedom of choice. But she cannot turn off her subconscious mind. This part of herself remains in touch with the reality involved. *The subconscious mind is never sophisticated.*

Thus, later in life, often during menopause, the deep psychic damage of a long-ago abortion might begin to surface. Dr. James C. Neely, author of *Gender,* says, "Repression we now know is more common than not after abortion, and we know that repression sooner or later will surface as psychic complaints."[6]

Regarding the effect of abortion on women, Dr. Howard W. Fisher, a Minneapolis psychiatrist, said that more data is needed, but that the physicians participating in abortion prevent the keeping of records that might contain the data.[7] No one is demanding to know. Nobody wants to know.

Everything you always wanted to know about sex, but don't want to know about abortion is a cultural syndrome. In this mental condition, women are trying to control what they perceive as enemies of their freedom, their own bodies, and making blind choices as if freedom depends on ignorance. In the meantime, men are profiting both sexually and financially. And women continue to look the other way.

18

Are Women Controlling Their Own Minds?

When choices are made in an environment that protects unawareness, the mind that makes the choices becomes extremely vulnerable. A woman's unknowing mind is easily taken over by a hard masculine mentality so that she thinks with the overly masculinized side of her mind and believes she is thinking in her own natural way.

This is what happens when she steps into the masculine trap. She begins to see control not as regulation from within but as domination from without. She sees nature in an extremely masculine way as an object to manage, conquer, and even exploit according to the desires and whims of the domineering controller.

The masculine and feminine ways of relating with nature are equally good. But an extreme masculine attitude is unhealthy. An extreme feminine attitude is equally disoriented.

Careful dominion is a wholesome masculine attitude. Raw domination is a harmful extreme. We need to see—clearly—the difference between dominion and domination-approaches to control.

Receptivity (listening to nature's requirements) is a wholesome feminine attitude. Inert passivity and chosen ignorance are negative and inhuman.

When masculine and feminine qualities do not interpenetrate and balance each other, they tend to break down into their negative extremes. A wholesome dominion breaks down into a domineering attitude. Strength deteriorates into hardness. Receptivity falls into passivity and blindness. Tenderness corrupts into softness.

Peering into the masculine trap where we see the minds of American women held captive, what lineaments can we bring to light? What cultural forces are controlling women's minds as well as their bodies?

19

Puritan and Playboy Mentalities

American culture is shaped by a largely unbalanced masculine mentality that has two basic forms: the puritan and the playboy philosophies of life. The puritan mentality has originated, and still forms, the American character. No other nation on earth was conceived, born, and developed in puritanism. Even the more recent playboy mentality, while strikingly different in some ways, remains basically puritan in its extremely masculine and domineering attitude toward nature.

The original puritan believed that he was fallen and depraved by sin, and that all the rest of nature shared this condition. He thought he could manage fallen nature only by force and domination.

The playboy, with one exception, agrees that nature should be dominated. This exception is physical sexuality and its psychological preferences. He thinks sex is absolutely good and almost incapable of immoral expression.

He also thinks that anything which might interfere with the fun of sex, such as pregnancy and emotional involvement, belongs to defective nature, and must be managed by domination. Instead of controlling his sexual *behavior* like the puritan, the playboy "liberates" his behavior and tries to control its unwanted *consequences* instead.

Puritan control of behavior and playboy control of consequences follow from the same inner problem. Neither the puritan nor the playboy knows how to live well with feelings.

The puritan hides his feelings, even from himself, because he thinks this will help him control his behavior. The playboy ignores his emotional feelings (especially those of bonding and love), because he thinks these interfere with freely chosen recreational sex. Hiding feelings and ignoring them are not the same. Yet both forms of domination show the same distorted masculine avoidance of feelings. Each, in its own way, says, "feelings don't count."

Living well with physical and emotional feelings requires something the puritan and playboy do not recognize in themselves—their inner receptivity. They do not accept the feminine aspect of their inner life.

Through the feminine part of ourselves (in both women and men), we are able to receive our feelings with awareness and acceptance of what they are. We are able to let them *be* what they are without having to *do* anything about them at all.

This ability to receive our feelings is also our capacity to regulate our behavior from within. If we can let ourselves have our sexual, angry, and other feelings without having to do what they suggest, we are really free to act or not to act. We do not feel driven to act. Nor do we feel driven to control ourselves by hiding or ignoring our feelings.

This inner freedom (to act or not to act no matter what we feel) changes the whole meaning of choice. It also changes the meaning of control from careless domination to caring dominion. Instead of suppressing or manhandling nature, we regulate it by receiving it deeply, and by freely cooperating with its principles of integrity.

When the masculine part of ourselves is unbalanced, we are not inclined to let anything just be itself. We feel compelled to produce and perform. Both the puritan work-ethic and the playboy fun-ethic accentuate performance in this excessive way. Success (in work or in sex) is their measure of self-worth. Simply being oneself causes too much anxiety.

The unreceived self tries to escape from itself precisely because it is unreceived. Doing something successfully is thought to prove the worth of a self not experienced otherwise as valuable from within. Doing (performance) becomes a flight from self, and, at the same time, a substituted validation for the unreceived self.

Rarely is an American male today a puritan or a playboy in the total sense. Each one, however, is affected by the mentalities that form the culture in which he lives. To the extent that individual males think and live by these mentalities, they are, partially at least, puritan and (or) playboy in character.

21

And to the degree that American females think and live by the same cultural attitudes, their own minds and lives are controlled by the mentalities of men. Their minds as well as their choices are not really their own.

CHAPTER THREE

WHAT WOMEN NEED TO KNOW ABOUT THEIR OWN MINDS

If women want to get out of the masculine trap, and stay out of the feminine mystique, they need to know themselves as female persons. They need to discover their own minds and develop their own mentality. And they need to know, with some clarity, the cultural attitudes that influence their minds so they can liberate themselves from mentalities not their own.

Without this knowledge and creative response, women cannot find a true solution to "the problem that has no name." Nor can they moderate and balance the masculine character of the world around and within them. Much less can they affect the masculine character of American culture and Western civilization.

By increasing their awareness, women can have a transforming influence. The future of the human family depends upon it. For example, the extreme masculine character of the nuclear weapons that remain erect and ready for planetary destruction signals an unprecedented need for mental balance. Actual release of these terrifying explosives to their targets would be a performance to end all performances. It would be masculine efficiency at its peak. It would be, at the same time, the ultimate impotence of extreme male power.

The need for a basic change in perspective is imperative. The great scientist, Albert Einstein, said, "The unleashed power of

23

the atom has changed everything except our ways of thinking. Thus we are drifting toward a catastrophe beyond comparison. We shall require a substantially new way of thinking if mankind is to survive."[1]

The power of women to help in developing this new way of thinking should not be overlooked, especially by women themselves. But many career-minded women today insist that the female mind is not different from the male mind, and that they have no uniquely feminine contribution to make.

Is their view correct? Or are they imposing a defensive (I'm just as good as you because I'm not different from you) ideology on themselves?

Female Minds, Male Minds

All of us have feminine and masculine aspects to our minds. For example, the global or holistic quality of intuition is feminine, and the linear or more focused quality of reason is masculine in both sexes.

Intuition and reason are usually organized in a more feminine way in female minds, however, and in a more masculine way in male minds.

Most women, not all, are spontaneously interested in who people are and how they are feeling. Men are spontaneously interested in what people do. They are more fascinated by occupations than by relationships, by projects and objects than by persons.

Diane McGuinness, a research psychologist at Stanford University, says that there are differences in the way males and females gather information and solve problems. "Men are more rule-bound, and they seem to be less sensitive to situational variables; more single-minded, more narrowly focused and more persevering. Women, by contrast, are *very* sensitive to context. They're less hidebound by the demands of a particular task. They're good at picking up peripheral information. And they

24

process the information faster. Put in general terms, women are communicators and men are takers of action."[2]

Many observers of these differences say they are due to upbringing, and have no biological foundation. But every one of the 30 billion cells in the female's brain, as well as in the rest of her body, has an XX set of sex chromosomes. And every cell in the male body and brain has an XY set of sex chromosomes. The brain is no exception to the general difference in the bodies of male and female.

By measuring electrical variations in the brain, researchers have discovered differences in responses to stimuli such as light and sound. They have found that women's brains are more responsive in every one of the senses tested and especially at higher levels of intensity.[3]

Investigators also say that sex hormones cause brain differences. Dr. Neely says in *Gender,* "Male and female hormones differentiate the sensory and motor processes at different rates and different times and this leads to certain nerve connections for boys and certain nerve connections for girls which, in turn, lead to varied behavior typical of the sex. In boys, this becomes rough-and-tumble play. In women, the emphasis is on fine movements, dexterity, and audiovisual sensitivity."[4]

The particular male emphasis on performance, as this emphasis appears throughout the animal kingdom, is vividly described by Jo Durden-Smith and Diane DeSimone, authors of *Sex and the Brain.* "Nature is full of chases, displays, dances, forced marches, obstacle courses, and other tests imposed on the male by the female. And it is clear that they are designed to deliver information not only about the male's genes, but also about his hormonal levels and his sperm capability...Can the male find food, build a nest or command a territory, and so pass the genes for these things down to a female's (male, at least) offspring? It is the quality of the male's inborn or partly learned performance that induces in the female's body the hormonal conditions necessary for a successful mating. If the male shows aggression or less than perfect skill in any part of his performance, the female brain can often shut down production of the messenger hormones that govern the delivery of her eggs."[5]

Though the human kingdom is vastly different in perspective and function from the animal kingdom, the human male is still wired for performance and efficiency more than the female. This is something that women need to know and to take into consideration.

When women realize that the male mind is more oriented than their own toward performance, efficiency, projects, and objects, they will not be so easily drawn into, and trapped by, a male way of thinking and acting. As a result, they can become more efficient at balancing the male way with the female way, and at integrating their own way with the male's without falling blindly into it.

A Different Organization of the Brain

Toward the purpose of uniting distinct minds without obliterating either of them, women need to know still more complex basics about the organization of the brain. They need to know that the brain of both sexes has two lobes or hemispheres, each specializing in a different way. The left hemisphere is logical and analytic. The right is intuitive, imaginative, and creative. The left side thinks; the right knows. The left specializes in verbal and language skills, the right in visual and spatial skills. The right side also processes emotions, such as reading the emotional content of tones of voice and facial expressions.[6]

Because the right side of the brain is intuitive and emotionally aware, it is more feminine in character than the left side. The logical left seems masculine by comparison. But something goes on between the two sides that appears, at first, to confuse this picture.

Scientific studies show that the masculine, or left, side of the brain which specializes in language develops more quickly and remains predominant, not in males as expected, but in females. And the feminine, or right, side which specializes in visual-spatial skills develops more quickly and remains predominant in males.

Apparently each side of the brain has a subdominant part connected in a special way to the opposite side. For instance, language from the left expresses emotions from the right; this is a more feminine use of words. Language from the left also expresses objective reasons from the left; this is a more masculine use of words. Thus, left-side language has both feminine and masculine purposes.

The female's mind puts left-side language at the service of right-side intuitions and feelings very early in life in a way that makes her more verbal in interpersonal relationships than males. Males are more inclined to put left-side language at the service of their left-side, more objective, interests.

According to the evidence, language is deployed in the left side of the male's brain in a pattern somewhat different from that in the female's brain. This suggests different neural wiring for language in males and females. The visual-spatial part of the right hemisphere also shows different male and female patterns.[7]

While females reach into the masculine side of the brain to get the language needed to express something going on in the feminine side, males reach into the feminine side to get the visual-spatial perceptions needed to express the more objective interests of their masculine side. The power behind the cross-over is the masculine side of the brain in the male, and the feminine side in the female. The apparent muddling of the two sides is only superficial.

When visual-spatial perceptions in the right side of the brain are put at the service of intuition and imagination, also in the right side, the results of this feminine pattern are things like art and music. But when visual-spatial perceptions are put at the service of linear logic and objective focus in the left side of the brain, the results of this masculine pattern are things like mathematics and mechanics.

Predominance of one side of the brain in females, and of the other side in males, shows that the brain is organized differently in the sexes. Evidence also shows less hemisphere specialization in females, and less separation between the two sides. Males have more concentration of a skill in one side of the brain. This is why damage to one side is more incapacitating to males than to females.[8]

Men do not express their feelings verbally as much, or as well as, women because they lack the amount of connection between the verbal left and the emotional right that women have. Researchers have found that the elongated bundle of fibers that carries information between the two halves of the brain—the corpus callosum—is wider and larger at the back of the brain in women than in men, and that this difference can be found in the developing brain before birth.[9]

The greater connection between feelings and words in women is found not only in the way the female brain is organized, but also in the way the mother-child relationship is organized. Male and female children have different emotional experiences with their mothers. Daughters are more like their mothers, and do not have to go through the emotional separation boys experience in finding their identity outside the mother-child relationship.

In this necessary process of developing one's identity, boys need to leave some of their feelings behind. They need to "separate" themselves from their feelings in a way girls do not. As a result, relationships and emotional intimacy (talking about feelings) are easier for girls. And individuality and performance are more important for boys.[10]

Brain organization and the earliest organization of human relationships thus support each other. The girl is more organized for empathy, and for talking about feelings and personal interests. The boy is more organized for moving away, not only from the femaleness of his mother into his own maleness, but also away from the feelings involved. In moving away from feelings, he is more inclined to move into performance and achievement.

28

Jerre Levy, a biopsychologist at the University of Chicago, speculates in an interesting way about the brain organization involved in male-female differences. She says, "The hemispheres of male brains are specialists—they speak different languages, verbal and visual-spatial. And it may be that they can communicate with each other only in a formal way, after encoding into abstract representations. The hemispheres of female brains, on the other hand, don't seem to be such specialists. And they *may* be able to communicate in a much less formal, less structured and more rapid way. If this is so, then it's entirely possible that females are much better than males at integrating verbal and nonverbal information."[11]

Because there is more communication between the hemispheres in the female brain, the two sides have a more intuitive, cooperative, and integrative relationship than they have in the male brain. While the male brain is more adept at taking things apart (analysis), the female brain is more adept at quickly fitting all sorts of peripheral information into a complete picture.

The female brain tends to arrive at the same conclusions as the male brain by skipping steps in the reasoning process. Men often call this skip-step kind of thinking "irrational." But there is more than one way of being rational. Step-by-step, or straight-line, reasoning is not the only way. Intuitive reasoning is just as rational as linear reasoning, though different.

Having less communication between them, the two sides of the male brain are more diverse in the way they function. They do not cooperate as well as the two sides in the female brain. *One advantage of less cooperation is more efficiency in performance.*

The female brain, by being more tuned-in to the emotional life, is more affective than effective. The female brain can also be very effective. The difference is simply a matter of emphasis.

Commenting on this emphasis, Sandra Witelson, a neuropsychologist, says, "Men appear better at doing two cognitive jobs at the same time, if the jobs depend mainly on different hemispheres, like talking and route-finding while driving, and women appear better at *single* cognitive jobs which require cooperation and communication *between* the two hemispheres, like reading or assessing a person on the basis of both verbal and visual cues."[12]

The ability to do two diverse tasks at once is, in a way, more effective than the ability to do one task that brings together different things. Integration tends to get in the way of efficiency, but in a good and necessary way. For example, the technology for nuclear war shows raw efficiency in a way that is stark and frightening. This efficiency is reduced when it is modified by a sensitive perception of life on this planet. Modified by more feminine concerns, nuclear technology can then be directed into life enhancing purposes.

Just as the XY pattern of the sex chromosomes in the male shows diversity between X and Y, the organization of the male brain shows diversity between the two hemispheres. By contrast, the XX pattern in the female shows similarity between the two Xs, and also more similarity between the two sides of the brain.

The XY brain differentiates better than it integrates. And the XX brain integrates better than it differentiates. Each mind can do what the other does, but with a unique gender orientation.

Two Orientations

The female mind has a special gift for uniting different things because its organization usually emphasizes the feminine power for seeing the whole in its parts. The masculine side of the mind sees, instead, the parts within the whole. If these two sides are not balancing each other, in women as well as in men, both sides fall into serious distortions. The feminine side by itself fails to distinguish the parts. And the masculine side by itself fails to see the whole.

Without the feminine side of the mind, Humpty Dumpty has a great fall into all his parts, and nothing can put him back together again.

The masculine gift for analysis separates a whole into its parts. Knowing that these parts came from a whole, the masculine mind wants to work out a synthesis. But it cannot succeed if it works by itself.

There is a false kind of synthesis that takes one of the parts, makes a new whole out of it, then tries to fit all the other parts into this first one. Freud tried this kind of synthesis when he reduced human energy to physical sexual energy, and then tried to explain everything else about human nature in the light of that one part. This false kind of synthesis is called reductionism.

Both the feminine and masculine sides of the mind have a sense of the whole, but in different ways. Consider, for a moment, the inside and outside of a hollow sphere. Both are sides of the same whole sphere. If you were inside the sphere, its wholeness would look one way to you. If you were outside, its wholeness would look quite different.

The kind of wholeness that is seen by the feminine side of the mind is something like the inside of a sphere. And the kind that is seen by the masculine is something like the outside of that same sphere.

We can see more of the outside of a sphere at once than we can see of the inside at once. Actually, we "sense" or intuit the wholeness of the inside before we see it.

Our hand can reach out to grasp the outside of a sphere. But we cannot reach out to grasp it inside. All we can do inside the sphere is touch and receive.

If we reach out to grasp an object from the outside, while we have no presence to that being from within its reality, we are going to break it down into its parts, and not really know how to see it in its wholeness again.

This is what happened to much of Western thinking. The Western mind cut itself off from its feminine side, and ended up with heaps of alienated systems.

The masculine side of the mind is gifted for specialization, diversification, and analysis. Its straight-line, step-by-step logic facilitates control. The feminine side is gifted for uniting diverse

31

elements. Its more global or intuitive logic facilitates cooperation and integration.

The feminine side of the mind is more inclined to unite opposites than to separate them. This ability to unite opposites can, for example, help a person become strong and tender at once. Men who think that they have to be strong and controlling, and rarely, if ever, tender, and women who think they have to be soft and tender, and not assertive or strong, are both thinking in a linear, overly masculine way. Both are thinking with a logic of identity (strong is strong, and tender is tender) and separation (men are strong, and women are tender).

The feminine ability to receive and to unite opposites is more inclined to see the paradoxes of reality. There are positive paradoxes that unite opposites (like tenderness and strength) that are valuable to each other. Tenderness and strength balance each other so they do not degenerate into softness and hardness. Negative paradoxes (softness and hardness: as personal characteristics) are more like contradictions that result from a lack of integration.

Paradoxical thinking, in the positive sense, helps men to be tender in their strength, and women to be strong in their tenderness. It also helps them to realize that men and women are not the same in strength or in tenderness, but that they emphasize these qualities in different, mutually enhancing, ways.

An inability to do integrative thinking appears in the ways people often interpret the relation between sex and procreation. At one time, many *identified* sex with procreation. Now many *separate* the two.

Neither approach is sound. A truly receptive mind sees that sex and procreation are neither identical nor separate, but are different parts within a single whole.

The part of the mind that sees wholeness from within fosters unity instead of separate compartments. The other part of the mind that sees wholeness from the outside is valuable for analysis, science, and technology. By itself, however, the outside-viewing part is incapable of finding its way back to the original whole. It is incapable of true synthesis.

Technology is linear, and focused toward a goal. Wisdom, more global in its perception, sees all of life as a balanced whole. Technology is concerned about *doing*. Wisdom is concerned about *being;* it is receptive and deeply thoughtful and does not have to do anything in order to be. Balancing technology with wisdom is a whole-brained way of using our minds, not just a half-brained emphasis.

The side of the mind that perceives wholeness from within calls the masculine side back from analysis to synthesis, from science and technology to wisdom. And both sides cooperate in the intercourse of a co-creative awareness.

The female mind usually emphasizes the receptive, integrative aspect of human awareness. And the male mind usually emphasizes the action-oriented, controlling and analytic aspect. Women and men have different orientations. They are meant to work together as the right and left hands of a person do. Each hand can do what the other does, but each is turned in a different direction.

If you would imagine your right hand on your left arm, you would see how different your right and left hands really are, though they also have ways in which they are the same. While being very much alike, your hands are differently oriented. If they were identical in orientation, they could not do things together, supporting and cooperating with each other. A person who would have two right hands, or two left hands, would severely miss this difference in orientation.

What a Culture Can Do

A culture that stresses the male organization of the mind develops a masculine character. This culture values the objective and controlling power of the mind far more than the holistic thinking that includes the person who knows.

In a masculinized way of seeing life, science becomes more important than wisdom. Wisdom might not be valued at all.

33

Science becomes transformed excessively into technology: science that works or performs. A culture that cuts itself off from the intuitive depths of the mind and emphasizes rational and technological awareness in education overemphasizes the masculine side of the minds it educates, including the minds of women.

In such an unbalanced culture, both men and women suffer. They sense a profound lack of wholeness.

Men are able to get along well enough, often without knowing, or even suspecting, that they are suffering. Women suffer more, and with more awareness of the lack of equilibrium. Eventually, they start complaining about their frustrations, and demanding some kind of answer.

The answer begins with an awareness of what is causing the frustration. What in the culture is at the bottom of the problem?

In other words, what is that culture's basic mentality? Men need to know as well as women. Then both can assess the situation and decide what to do about it.

The Power of a Mentality

At the bottom of a culture's character is its mentality. This quality of mind is like the air we breathe. It is all around us and within us. Usually subconscious as well as conscious, our mentality is the way we think and live.

We can have a way of thinking and living without even knowing what it is. We can be largely controlled by a mental system that operates in our subconscious minds. How many of us, who are functioning harmoniously in American culture today, can actually say what frame of mind this culture has and where it came from?

Whatever we think about God, even if we are atheists, forms the most influential part of our mentality. Whatever we think about the world and ourselves forms the rest of our perspective.

Every area of our mentality colors and affects all other areas. But none does this as much as our attitude about God.

If it is true, as *Genesis* says, that we are made in the image and likeness of God, we are destined to identify with our view of God probably more than we realize. For instance, as we shall see later, the puritan view of God formed the puritans' character, and consequently the character of the culture they founded.

Once a mentality is established in a culture, it tends to persist for centuries. A world-view tends to affect a culture and its people long after its cause recedes from the surface of history and goes underground.

In the subconscious life of a nation and its people, an "old" mentality remains alive while new ones rise and recede. The apparently passé perspective remains active in shaping and nuancing what seems to be, at the time, a new way of thinking and living.

An "old" mentality even tends to increase in power the deeper it goes into the underground. This growth in power happens precisely because people forget the original world-view that formed their culture, and do not realize that this subconscious milieu could be more influential now than ever.

The only thing that can break the hypnotic spell of a culture's underground and background mind-set is a clear, unforgetting awareness of its presence and character.

Women, and men too, need to become clearly aware of the extremely masculine mentality that holds our culture, and ourselves, in its power. Culture-awareness of this kind involves, for Americans, special attention to the original view of reality (the puritan view) that formed us as a people. Women, especially, need this awareness if they want to exit the masculine trap, avoid a return to the feminine mystique, and finally think and live according to their own true selves.

PART TWO

THE PROBLEM'S PROGRESS

CHAPTER FOUR

THE PURITAN AIR WE BREATHE— OVERLY MASCULINE

In our usual image of the puritans, we see the Mayflower, its landing at Plymouth Rock, the Massachusetts Bay Colony, and the first Thanksgiving feast. We see how serious these people were, how moral and religious, how powerful in their purposes. We sense their heroism and their strong dedication to liberty. With some reservations about their austerity, we are proud that they are the archetypes of our national character.

Though the original puritans disappeared long ago, their spirit lives on. Their ideals permeate the air we breathe. Daniel Bell, a cultural historian, says, "It is the character of ideologies...once launched, to take on a life of their own...Unlike economies or outmoded technologies, they do not disappear...This was the fate of Puritanism. Long after the harsh environment that fostered the initial ideology had been mitigated, the force of the belief remained."[1]

Having a clear sense of the power a mentality can have over centuries of history, Sydney Ahlstrom, a professor of American History at Yale University, calls the time from Queen Elizabeth (1558) to the election of John F. Kennedy (1960) "a Great Puritan Epoch." Ahlstrom does not mean that puritanism explains everything that happened in this span of time. He does mean, though, that the puritan impulse, through all its changes in

39

form, remained the dominant factor in the ideology of America's Protestant Establishment. All other elements among the people—Catholic, Orthodox, Jewish, infidel, red, yellow and black—had to relate, in some way, to the puritan tradition.[2]

The puritan epoch, however, is far from over. In spite of a Catholic becoming president in a puritan nation, the puritan mentality persists. Kennedy's political thinking was influenced more by the Establishment than by his religion, and did very little to change the American character.

The Absence of the Feminine

Though the original puritans were passionately religious, there was nothing feminine about their sense of God and themselves. Their religious perceptions lacked warmth and intimacy. Their extremely masculine mentality saw God as cold and remote.

Religious intensity is not the same as spiritual vitality. The spiritual life is feminine as well as masculine. It is intuitive, receptive, warm, and intimate as well as discerning, motivated, courageous, and outgoing.

Spiritually sensitive people value love more than achievement, fidelity more than success, and cooperation more than competition. They have a vital sense of cooperation with God, with nature, and with other people.

Though the puritans fervently honored and obeyed God, they lacked a feeling for intimate sharing with God. They saw God through Calvinist eyes as a demanding lawgiver, and human nature as absolutely depraved by sin.

A depraved self under a demanding lawgiver is more likely to feel emotional and spiritual distance than warmth and love.

The great New England puritan mind of Jonathan Edwards dramatizes the situation. In his sermon "Sinners in the Hands of an Angry God," he told his congregation:

You are thus in the hands of an angry God. It is nothing but his mere pleasure that keeps you from being this moment swallowed up in everlasting destruction....The God that holds you over the pit of hell, much as one holds a spider, or some loathsome insect over the fire, abhors you, and is dreadfully provoked: his wrath towards you burns like fire; he is of purer eyes than to bear to have you in his sight; you are ten thousand times more abominable in his eyes than the most hateful venomous serpent is in ours....There is no other reason to be given, why you have not dropped into hell since you arose in the morning, but that God's hand has held you up. You hang by a slender thread, with the flames of divine wrath flashing and ready every moment to singe it, and burn it asunder; and you have no interest in any Mediator, and nothing to lay hold of to save yourself, nothing to keep off the flames of wrath, nothing of your own, nothing that you ever have done, nothing that you can do, to induce God to spare you one moment.[3]

Such an attitude is mightily religious. But it is not very spiritual. God is too remote for spiritual intimacy, too wrathful for cooperation, and we are too close to hell and far from heaven for spiritual joy.

Where did this tragic sense of religion come from? Why was the warm, feminine aspect of the spirit fading away? Why were these Christians losing their Gospel sense of God as a hen gathering *her* young beneath *her* wing (Luke 13:34)?

Before the puritans came along, and even earlier, before the Protestant Reformation of the 16th century, Christians began feeling a chill in the spiritual atmosphere. They were becoming more world-aware. Works of art started showing landscapes. The first artist able to show people standing firmly on the ground was Masaccio, an early 15th century painter.

Along with this more earthly awareness came a new sense of the human self. At the same time, trust in God's love went down as a feeling of the self's inability to measure up to the Father's demands went up.

Anxiety about salvation increased. Like any kind of chronic anxiety, salvation-anxiety triggered a defensive reaction. The defense became an extreme effort to *get saved* by performing good works (celibacy, penances, and pilgrimages), not as means of union with God, but to gain indulgences, or to attain a higher place in heaven.

When the feminine side of salvation weakened, the masculine side came on stronger. When faith and trust lessened, human efforts took on more importance. Good works were valued more than faith. Performing became more important than receiving. The masculine side of the soul took over and began suppressing the feminine.

Eventually, some salvation-anxious Christians began to sense futility in their religious efforts. Martin Luther (1483-1546) was one of them. He felt incapable of good works without pride and imperfection. Finally, he believed that salvation comes through faith alone, and that human nature is too deformed by sin to be capable of good works that have saving merit.

Instead of restoring the feminine aspect of the spiritual life, Luther's interpretation of faith repressed the feminine. He based faith on what he thought was the radical passivity of human nature, instead of its active receptivity.

Luther's interpretation of faith also took the spiritual power of good works away from the masculine side of human nature. Without receptivity (an active receiving of divine grace) there could be no meritorious activity or good works having salvation value, not even by cooperating with God's grace.

Even after salvation replaces the "old Adam" with the "new Adam," the new Adam, according to Luther, still has *no power* to engage in spiritually meritorious action. This total lack of power in anything directed toward heaven turns Christian attention toward the earth, and into highly active religious efforts such as preaching the Bible to save souls, to strengthen their faith, and to build the Kingdom of God here in this world.

42

Religious Intensity,
Spiritual Impotence

Going still further down the road of nature's perceived depravity and helplessness, John Calvin (1509-1564) thought that people are not even saved by faith, but only by predestination. According to Calvin, only the few who are favored by God's arbitrary choice can be saved.

In relation to this divine choice, there is absolutely nothing an individual can do to be saved, not even believe. The human person is spiritually impotent. As Jonathan Edwards said, "Nothing you can do can induce God to spare you one moment." The chilling of the spiritual atmosphere that began before the Reformation was now complete.

A Wanting and Unwanting God

In the purely Calvinist sense, predestination means that the totally depraved, inert, impotent, human being is either chosen or condemned by God "according to the good pleasure of God's own will." The God of predestination does not make choices motivated by his own goodness or wisdom, but simply by his own absoluteness.[4] The individual is neither able to make the choice of salvation himself, nor to cooperate with God in working out that choice. Only by being already chosen can the elect experience the effects of grace which God offers them in return for their faith.[5]

This view was a proposed answer to the anxiety about salvation that preceded Luther. Ironically, it was also a return to that same anxiety in another form. People were forced to wonder, "Am I saved or not? Am I one of the elect? I just don't know. And what is worse, there is simply nothing I can do about it." Salvation was, for them, an obsessive worry. Where was the warm, affirming "hen" that would gather under her wing all who would come?

The American puritans, as well as some of the English puritans, were Calvinists. They were convinced that each individual is either mercifully chosen as one of the elect (the wanted) or else mercilessly doomed (the unwanted). They believed they themselves were chosen, and others were unwanted by their God. This bothered some of the American puritans. They argued and disagreed among themselves about predestination. Some interpreted it less harshly than others.[6]

Their wanting and unwanting Lord was a God of power, governance, and sovereignty—absolutely inscrutable in his ways. This God was "entirely incomprehensible, hidden, unknowable, and unpredictable."[7]

So much remoteness and distance could not encourage spiritual intimacy. A God so unknowable says little about God, but much about the spiritual alienation of people who have such a perception of God.

The Performance Reaction

Though the puritans probably did not know it consciously, their spiritual inability to do anything basic about their salvation generated in them a powerful masculine reaction. Extreme passivity in one area of the self makes the same self try to compensate for this "blank space" by generating extreme activity in another area of the self.

In other words, the negative feminine aspect of inertness generates the negative masculine aspect of excessive activity. In the puritans, this masculine reaction to their spiritual passivity became their driven work-and-performance ethic.

Forced to wonder "Am I one of the elect?" the Calvinists, including the puritans, wanted some kind of proof. Without it they could have no peace of mind.

Some Calvinists thought the proof was to be found in a morally righteous life and in productive work. The puritans agreed. And so they "performed diligently in all of their secular roles, just as they were conscientious in the performance of their religious duties. They rejected the excesses in which so many of their fellow men indulged and imposed a rigid discipline upon themselves and their families."[8]

Some American Calvinists thought that assurance of salvation appears in economic success as well as in moral righteousness. They believed that the well-off are probably wanted by God, and that the poor and unsuccessful probably are unwanted and destined for hell. Needless to say, this view became an unprecedented religious boost for capitalism.

Behind the high achievement (masculine) drive of the puritans was their total spiritual helplessness. Unable to cooperate with God in working out their eternal salvation, they would work out, instead, their earthly salvation. And their success in working out their earthly salvation would prove to themselves and others that they were, indeed, among the Chosen.

In this way, the religious anxiety of the puritans became a driving force behind their tremendous political, scientific, and economic accomplishments. Their subconscious, if not conscious, reaction against their spiritual powerlessness became emotional energy for their work, and eventually, a powerful "steam engine" for the Industrial Revolution.

The puritan approach to work, to the extent that it was driven by an intense spiritual anxiety, was a futile attempt to fill the void of the ignored, or even feared, feminine side of human nature. Work was valued at the expense of warmth and intimacy. It began to interfere with relationships. Instead of experiencing work as a way of cooperating with God, with nature, and with other people, the puritans often experienced work as a solitary way of proving to themselves that they were saved.

Alienated in a deep spiritual way from God, from nature, and from other people, the puritans cut themselves off from the feminine side of human nature in other ways as well. Except for the Bible, they rejected religious tradition. They left their mother country and sailed across a vast ocean to start new colonies and eventually a new nation. The Industrial Revolution, a result of the puritan work-ethic, treated Mother Nature not as a home to be cherished and respected, but as a resource for an age of production.

Tough Individualism

As with all other aspects of the puritan mentality, puritan individualism had a distinctly religious source. When the puritans centered the Church in the Bible, reversing the traditional centering of the Bible in the Church, each individual became an interpreting authority for the Bible. That was a giant step into religious individualism, one made possible by the invention of the printing press and the subsequent distribution of Bibles to the common people.

Religious individualism soon became a quality of character that affected everything else in puritan life. The ideal became the tough, resourceful, independent, invulnerable individual who could take care of himself against all odds. This ideal generated the philosophy of the self-made man.

Beginning with Luther's "Here I stand," and leading to Walt Whitman's "I am the master of my fate, the captain of my soul," the overly-masculine sense of the individual reached its peak in the American character. Tough individualism made possible survival in the wilderness, not only in New England, but in all the other American frontiers.

The Masculine Era

More than a century before Luther and Calvin, a masculine type of consciousness started to take hold of civilization in the

46

Renaissance. The Reformation gave this masculine emphasis a powerful religious reinforcement.

Paul Tournier, a Swiss psychiatrist, describes the basic situation as follows:

> There took place at the Renaissance and at the beginning of the modern age a great psychological event: a choice, to the disadvantage of feeling and to the advantage of reason, to the prejudice of the body and the profit of the intellect, at the expense of the person in favor of things. Much more—a kind of repression took place: the repression of affectivity, of sensitivity, of the emotions, of tenderness, of kindness, of respect for others, of personal relationship, of mystical communion- and of woman, with whom all the terms in this list are linked by spontaneous association of ideas. Such is our modern Western world, advanced, powerful, efficient, but cold, hard, and tedious; a world in which diseases accessible to objective study are vanquished, but in which neuroses related to lack of love are multiplied; in which we have amassed a great wealth of things, while the quality of life has deteriorated. The quality of life belongs to a different order, that of feeling.[9]

The part played in this history by Calvinism and the puritans was basic and profound. The autonomous self that resulted could not be the same as the wholeness of the person. A masculine type of self-awareness, when it is cut off from the feminine side of the person, cannot be whole.

Descartes, a French philosopher of the 17th century, was filled with this extremely masculine awareness. His solitary and self-conscious "I think therefore I am," followed Calvin's solitary and self-conscious "I wonder whether I am saved." The cold, distant (deist) God of the Enlightenment, following Calvin's hard, cold, remote lawgiver, was exclusively (and therefore extremely) masculine, lacking all personal presence and intimacy.

47

The Calvinist mentality, especially in its secularized form, gradually filled the air of Western civilization. And many civilized minds, often without knowing it, "breathed" this air.

The new, masculine consciousness produced good, as well as distorted, results. The time was right for a new sense of the individual person to emerge in history, though not in the extreme form that it did. The need was great for science to develop, but only in the context of wisdom. Civilization was ready for new social, political, and economic developments, though not at the expense of human relationships.

The wonderful gifts of the masculine era were, and still are, incomplete. They lack the feminine aspect of consciousness that still waits to emerge.

Architects of Liberty

Probably because the God of predestination was experienced as such a willful and tyrannizing monarch, the puritan spirit felt a subconscious revulsion against monarchy. The puritans then expressed this (hidden) negative reaction against the divine monarch, first by rejecting religious monarchy (the papacy) in Europe, then later, by rejecting civil monarchy (the king of England) in America.

There was, however, another side to the God of predestination, one not rejected, but wholeheartedly accepted. The divine sovereign was also a lawgiver. Combining their rejection of monarchy with their great respect for law, the puritans (especially those of the 18th century, such as John Locke and Benjamin Franklin) became social and political innovators. They became great architects of liberty based on law. They saw to it that the supposedly stable rule of law replaced the often arbitrary rule of kings. The result, in our country, is our constitutional and democratic form of government.

At the time of the Revolutionary War, the ministers of New England often spoke about political subjects in their sermons.

They were so interested in the Biblical concept of liberty that their religion became political.

For the puritan ministers, the cornerstone of liberty was the Bible.[10] The biblical image of the Hebrews leaving bondage and entering the Promised Land was especially significant for them. They loved the liberating words, "You shall know the truth and the truth shall make you free."

In their sermons, the parsons favored revolutions that yielded freedom, but only freedom based on law. They were staunch believers in compacts, constitutions, and Magna Chartas.[11]

Some students of puritanism[12] think that the idea for the American Constitution actually came from the puritan theology of the Covenant. In other words, they think that political ideas came from religious ideas.

Even if Locke and Jefferson never quoted their religious sources (few people advert to the air they breathe), the theology of the Covenant certainly influenced their ideas about the social compact and constitutional government. (An agreement between individualists that they will all follow the same law formed a social kind of covenant that made a constitutional government possible.) And a Constitution that establishes checks and balances was certainly influenced by the puritan concept of depravity in everyone, including those in power. The idea seemed to be that human perversity demands built-in restraints *on leaders* as well as on everyone else.

The puritan religion was thus a generator of new political and secular movements. Sydney Ahlstom goes so far as to say that puritanism virtually sacrificed itself on the altar of civic responsibility. "It helped to create a nation of individualists who were also fervent 'moral athletes,' with a strong sense of transcendent values which must receive ordered and corporate expression in the commonwealth."[13]

Even Jonathan Edwards, a fiery preacher of the Great Awakening (1720-1740), whom many regard as the greatest theologian in American history,[14] had a secularizing influence. He was an avid student not only of Calvinism but also of science and the secularizing Enlightenment. He led many "down a path that would create a revolution and a new nation just as surely as would the natural rights philosophy of other colonists."[15]

At the bottom of the matter, religious intensity without spiritual potency was destined to convert itself into secular impulses. Though Luther did not say it in these words, his message came down to this: "You cannot do anything to climb higher in heaven, so you might as well put your energies into improving the earth. And because no one can do anything to climb higher in heaven than anyone else, all men are equal."[16]

It took some time for this Reformation-mentality to bring about the American form of government. But the result was quite inevitable. The secularizing and democratizing effect of Luther's stance moved steadily along through Calvinism into puritanism, and from there into the foundations of the American republic.

In spite of periods of cultural change, the puritan ideals of individualism, freedom, achievement, practicality and free enterprise have dominated the American character to this day. This distinctive set of virtues stands as a great human accomplishment. But, because of its one-sided, exaggerated masculine emphasis, it was attained at the expense of human wholeness.

The New Woman and the Puritan Mentality

Puritan women were industrious, thrifty, practical, domestic, and submissive to their husbands. Their status was raised by the Protestant combination of romantic love with marriage. At the same time they were limited to marriage and the family by the Protestant exclusion of religious celibacy as an honored choice for women.

Previously, romantic love was an affair of the heart, usually directed outside of marriage, and was not supposed to be genitally involved. Romanticism made the woman a lady and "put her on a pedestal," a historic phase in raising the status of women.

Puritanism, by combining romantic love with sex in marriage, took women off the pedestal, still treated them as ladies, and gave them more equality with their husbands than was previously the case. But puritan women, confined to domestic life, had little effect on the performance mentality that shaped the civilization at large.

In the 1950s and 60s, when women started to complain about "the problem that has no name," four things were beginning to happen, mostly subconsciously. Women were reacting against the excessively masculine character of their culture. They were feeling a need to break out of the "feminine mystique" that imprisoned them in the domestic realm. They were sensing a need to develop the masculine side of their minds in a woman's way, not a man's. And they were feeling a need to develop a feminine way of thinking, not just a feminine way of living.

Women were subconsciously, if not consciously, longing to contribute the feminine insights of the mind to the advancement of a civilization that urgently needed more balance and wholeness. But, as explained earlier, many women failed to interpret their situation correctly. The answer they sought in jobs and careers became a temporary distraction from the nameless problem that later would return to disturb them again.

The new work-oriented, achieving, self-proving, wanting-and-unwanting female of the women's liberation movement reacted to her inner void by trying to fill it with the male's way of thinking. This reaction was not, and never will be, a true solution. The extremely masculine response to the feminine mystique was an unfortunate misstep. Women still need, as much as ever, liberation from an overly masculine control of their minds, hearts, and lives.

Translating Regine Pernoud, a historian specializing in women's history, Paul Tournier quotes her saying: "It is as if women, delighted with the idea of having penetrated the masculine world, remained incapable of the extra effort of imagination they need to make in order to endow that world with their own particular character, which is the very quality that our society lacks. They are content to imitate men, to be judged capable of doing the same jobs, to adopt the manners and even the sartorial habits of their partners....One begins to wonder if they are not moved by unconscious admiration...of a masculine world which they think it necessary and sufficient to copy as exactly as possible, even at the cost of losing their own identity and denying in advance their own originality."[17]

If women fail to discover their own identity and their own originality, it will not be possible to modify puritanism in America. Without a social movement in the feminine powers of human nature, the masculine powers cannot even be affected, much less changed. The masculine side of human nature, without the feminine side, will never balance itself anymore than the feminine without the masculine could.

A woman's desire to have a career for her own fulfillment, or for economic security and leverage in case she is abandoned by her husband, is authentic. But the new woman's idea that it is practically impossible to fulfill herself without a career in a man's world, and that she can prove her worth only in her achievements, is radically puritan. So, too, is her driven attitude toward work. She has hardly begun to challenge the puritan emphasis on performance and efficiency, or to put this emphasis in a more human perspective. She moves courageously into the male type of individualism that says, "I am the master of my fate, the captain of my soul." The self-made man becomes the self-made woman.

She sells herself completely to the masculine way when, following the example of the puritan God, she judges her own children as wanted and unwanted, and rids herself of the unwanted before they are born. The God of Predestination never had a more perfect image and likeness.

It is ironic that this hard, masculine, most perfect resemblance shows up more starkly in women than in men. The absence of the feminine in puritanism seems to take, in this grotesque way, its final revenge.

CHAPTER FIVE

PERFORMANCE SEXUALITY: FROM PURITAN TO PLAYBOY

The new woman's desire to have sex just like men shows how the male way of thinking affects her sexuality as well as her mind. She insists on her right to have sex as she pleases, free from all ties and consequences, even if she has to tie herself to the medical profession to get it that way.

Instead of copying the male's approach to sexuality, women need to discover their own sexuality. They need to tell men what they learn, and assertively expect men to acknowledge what they say.

This kind of challenge from women to men can help men develop their own sexuality. Though they might resist at first, many will be grateful later when they experience the liberation of more receptivity within themselves.

The puritan performance-mentality holds many American men in its grip. Unless women find a more balanced way of thinking and living, and through it, a more balanced sexuality, men do not have a chance for sexual wholeness. They will just stay where they are, especially if women continue to ignore their own inner selves by wanting sex just like men.

Men tend to assume that intimacy involves physical intercourse. Women tend to approach intimacy verbally and tactilely more than genitally. They expect real closeness to involve warm touching, sharing, and discussing their feelings and experiences.

Anne Wilson Schaef describes these orientations in a revealing story.

> I once saw a couple in therapy who exemplified these differences. Each had a different intimacy fantasy about their reconnection after an absence from each other. He traveled a great deal in relation to his work. As he approached home, his fantasy went like this: He would come home from the airport, walk through the front door, embrace his wife, take her directly into the bedroom, and they would make love. Then they would be connected and intimate with each other. Her fantasy went like this: He would walk through the door after his business trip, she would tell him everything she had been doing and thinking during his absence, and he would respond by telling her everything he had been doing and thinking while they were apart. She would share new insights and awarenesses and *so would he*. She would then be ready to make physical love. They might, or might not, but that decision would be made together. The important thing, to her, was that their intimate connection with each other had been established through mutual sharing.
>
> He experienced her words as a barrier to intimacy. She experienced his physical advances as a barrier to intimacy. When they came into therapy, they informed me that they had decided to seek help because of *her* sexual problem! Her husband had accused her of being frigid—and she had started to believe him![1]

Many men and some women do not realize that emotional and mental intercourse between a man and a woman is just as much sexual intercourse as genital union.

To begin with, every cell in the brain and heart of a man—in his whole body—has an XY set of sex chromosomes. And every cell in the entire body of a woman has an XX set of sex chromosomes. Men and women are sexually different in their entire humanity. A man is a man in his whole self, not just in

54

part of himself. A woman is a woman, too, in every part of herself, not only in her anatomy.

Intercourse of the brain and heart is just as sexual, though not as physical, as genital intercourse. In both men and women, sexual intercourse of the emotional and mental kind is meant to precede genital intercouse. Women just sense it more strongly.

Male reticence about verbalizing feelings in relationships does not mean that men lack verbal ability. They can be articulate communicators.

Men excel, however, in communication with objective intent, the kind that delivers a message and makes a point. Women have more aptitude for verbal sharing about subjective matters: feelings, intuitions, and personal relationships.

A sexual orientation that heads for performance without a deep sharing of thoughts and feelings short-circuits the emotional dynamism of human sexuality. Men can live with this state of affairs more easily than women. Women need to realize this clearly before they can find a better way for both themselves and men. They need to heighten their awareness by studying the performance-reaction in puritanism, and how this reaction affected, and still affects, men. Women need to know what "the air they breathe" is doing not only to men but also to themselves.

Puritan Sexuality

The sexuality of the Elizabethan and early American puritans was not repressed, as was the subsequent sexuality of the Victorians. But puritan sexuality was controlled and highly sublimated (much of their sexual energy was redirected into work). Strong romantic and passionate feelings often were expressed not in emotional intimacy or physical intercourse, but in social, economic, scientific, and cultural achievement.

The puritan attitude toward feelings was more negative than positive. According to their view, feelings belong to the

55

depravity of human nature. Adulterous feelings, not just adulterous decisions or actions, were regarded as totally evil.

All spontaneous feelings, including feelings such as anger and fear, are initially good because our nature is basically good. Feelings become defective—such as anger turned into resentment—only when we encourage and elaborate those that should not be encouraged. The result can be evil attitudes and decisions.

Sexual feelings, as they initially occur, provide energy for the inner development of one's manhood or womanhood. Simply accepting these feelings as energy for making morally good decisions is a way of developing one's sexuality. Relegating them, instead, to the pits of vileness greatly hinders the person's natural ability to *live well* with sexual feelings.

In spite of this problem with feelings, puritan sexuality represented a kind of sexual revolution, one that based marriage more on romantic love and companionship than on procreation. Previously, marriage was based on procreation, and it existed in the context of the extended family which included many relatives. Parents chose spouses for their children. Companionship between husband and wife was part of marriage, but was not as important in the extended family as it later became in the nuclear family: father, mother, and children as a more exclusive unit.

While the puritan revolution based marriage on husband-wife romantic love, it also helped to develop, at the same time, the nuclear family. Puritan individualism, by breaking up the communal sense of the extended family, brought about a new order in both marriage relationships and family life.

Traditional Christianity valued celibacy, and saw it as equal with marriage, although many theologians saw it as higher. Protestantism profoundly changed this view. Marriage became the most important way of life. Sexual intercourse became more important as an expression of love. And children remained a valued purpose of marriage, but no longer the main purpose.

Though marriage was not regarded as a sacrament, the family remained sacred. And the lord of the family was the husband/father/master, but because of the existence of mutual duties, the wife's position often approached equality with her husband in certain respects.[2] The husband was "prince and teacher, pastor and judge in his household....He was the legal representative of his family."[3]

In a new and good way, the puritans valued the sexual expression of love in marriage. Both their love and their sexuality were adversely affected, however, by their other characteristics. Their self-preoccupation, heavy moralism, and driven work-ethic had a cooling effect on their emotional intimacy, even though man-woman companionship received a new, positive emphasis in puritanism.

As the puritan was rechanneling his frustrated spiritual energy into work to assure himself of his salvation, he was also, at the same time, rechanneling his sexual energy into work for the same reason. This double overloading of his performance drive made him a superb producer, inventor, and achiever. It made him highly sublimated in the negative sense.

Because the feminine aspect of the spiritual life (a deep and active receptivity) was repressed, the feminine side of human sexuality (emotional warmth and intimacy) was regarded with suspicion and was negatively affected. The puritans were far too masculine in character to be models of human and sexual wholeness.

The Victorian Closet

Suspicious attitudes toward human nature and sexual feelings were strong enough in puritanism that Victorianism could come along and easily closet sex altogether. In the last half of the 19th and first part of the 20th century, puritan sublimation deteriorated into Victorian repression. The mentality became, "We can make evil go away if we simply refuse to look at it." This attitude of civilizing by ignoring was gaining acceptance as early as the 1820s, and was partly a reaction against the sexual looseness of the Napoleonic era.

The Victorian mentality tolerated sex for the sake of offspring. At its worst, the male was allowed to impregnate the female in a dark bedroom, while she endured it silently as if in a coma.

Sex was never to be mentioned anywhere. It was banned from polite conversation. The young were physically punished to keep their sexuality rigidly controlled. Fashions were changed to conceal women's bodies almost completely. Many people became sick with neurotic torments, and some became psychotic. Frightening warnings from physicians and from the pulpits helped keep sex in the closet.[4]

The Foot in the Door

Then, in 1900, Sigmund Freud got his foot into the closet door as he began to publish his views about the human psyche and the repressive cause of neurosis. In 1913, Margaret Sanger began to promote what she called, in masculine terms, birth control. Writers like Shaw, Conrad, and Lawrence were prying open the closet. No one pursued the liberation of sex as passionately and obsessively as D.H. Lawrence (*Sons and Lovers*, 1913; *Women in Love*, 1921), who came to the fore as Victorian moralism was losing its hold.

In 1915, some Harvard students known as The Young Intellectuals began reading Freud, Bergson, and Neitzsche.[5] Their thinking was influenced by the emphasis these authors put on instinct, vitality, and irrationality. They launched an attack on puritanism and Victorianism by openly promoting an ethic of hedonism, pleasure, and play. These young men were America's first "playboy" advocates of sexual liberation.

Less than a decade later, their impulse-ethic became part of what was then called the "new capitalism." The puritan age of work and production was shifting into the playboy age of recreation and consumption. By the 1920's, mass consumption was well on its way. It reached its peak in the 1950s and 1960s as the playboy culture shifted into high gear.

As the age of production based on *needs* expanded into the age of consumption based on *wants*, a culture of delayed gratification was gradually replaced by one of immediate gratification. Three capitalist innovations made this change possible: mass production on the assembly line, marketing and advertising, and payment in installments. Luxuries formerly reserved for the upper class were mass-produced for consumption by the middle and lower classes, and were redefined by advertising as necessities. Delayed payments encouraged impulse-buying which increased consumption.[6] People were expected to cultivate their *tastes* instead of their *values*.

But puritan values still haunted the consumer society. The corporation still motivated its employees to work hard, to achieve, and to delay gratification while on the job. At the same time, the corporation promoted instant gratification in its products and advertisements. The conflicting message became: "Produce and consume; be a puritan by day and a playboy by night."

Ways of attracting attention and manipulating the impulse to buy became necessary for increasing sales. Since nothing catches the attention of the consumer like sex, playmate figures posed with every kind of product from cleaners to Cadillacs. The display of women's bodies became a major selling technique. Sex was out of the closet and progressing toward blatancy on billboards and airwaves everywhere.

From Compulsive to Impulsive

When sex came out of the closet and moved onto mainstreet and the front page, a basic shift in cultural character took place. The compulsive character that runs on sheer willpower gave way to the impulsive character that spurns willpower and acts instead on impulses.

Both the compulsive and the impulsive are masculine extremes. Both are directed outward toward actions without an inner receptive attitude toward feelings. Neither of these masculine extremes knows how to live well with feelings and emotions.

Our feelings belong to the spontaneous part of ourselves, and need to be received as such. Feelings lead to impulses and impulses lead to actions. But we are free to choose whether or not our impulses will lead to actions. We do not have to act on our impulses. We can be responsible.

The responsible (response-able) part of ourselves is supposed to take care of the spontaneous part of ourselves as a parent takes care of a child. When the responsible part fails to *receive* feelings by affirming them as they are, we are locked into either of two extremes. Either we become too concerned about our behavior, or not concerned enough. We become moralistic and compulsive like the puritan, or non-moral and impulsive like the playboy.

The responsible part of ourselves is supposed to be both feminine and masculine: receptive toward our feelings (inner mothering) and firm in guiding our behavior (inner fathering).

When the feminine side of responsibility is absent, and the masculine side still tries to maintain itself, the latter tends to become extreme or compulsive. Then a healthy sense of morality is impossible; morality breaks down into moralism.

And when the feminine and masculine sides of responsibility are both absent, the spontaneous part of ourselves becomes impulsive. A healthy sense of morality is equally impossible. Morality breaks down into various shades of non-morality (including a neutral attitude) and immorality.

Sigmund Freud, the father of the cultural shift from the compulsive to the impulsive type of character, exposed moralism as a compulsive extreme. He did not intend to undermine morality. But he thought, wrongly, that morality comes mainly from a need for order in society. Instead, morality comes mainly from a need for order within each individual person.

Because of the faulty starting point of his thinking, Freud's view of morality contained the seeds of its own destruction. Subsequently, moralism led to its opposite extreme: no connection between sex and morality. Freud simply missed the receptive side of the mind that discovers and receives requirements for moral integrity within the nature of the human person.

Strongly influenced by the puritans and Victorians, Freud believed that human nature is basically evil. How, then, could he see human nature as a source of moral integrity? He could not.

But he did see that people need to live together in some kind of harmony, and that, for this purpose, social standards are necessary. According to Freud, society imposes its rules, mainly through parents, on what he called the superego. This part of the psyche makes the sexual instinct (the id) submit to social requirements. Submission is done either consciously, by suppressing feelings, or unconsciously, by repressing feelings.

Carefully interpreted, Freud's distinction between conscious and unconscious control is a valuable contribution. Suppression of some impulses, which is conscious, is part of a healthy sense of morality. Repression of feelings, which is unconscious, is part of moralism and is sick.

Impulses may be *suppressed*. But *spontaneous feelings* must not be *repressed*.

Besides suppression done simply for the sake of the social status quo, Freud also defended sublimation, which is done for the sake of social advancement. When sexual feelings are sublimated, they are used as energy, not for genital acts, but for artistic, political, and scientific achievements. Sexual energy is redirected into social progress and cultural development.

By defending suppression and sublimation for social purposes, Freud defended morality against impulsiveness. But his foundation for moral integrity was too weak to hold out against the blind surge of feelings and impulses that followed his overthrow of moralism.

Based on his negative convictions about human nature, Freud's view of both suppression and sublimation was largely negative. The one thing that could have made his view positive and that could have strengthened his sense of moral integrity (an inner feminine receptivity), was totally lacking in the starting point of his thinking. Understandably, then, the compulsive character he criticized soon moved into the impulsive character he did not advocate.

Wilhelm Reich, author of *The Sexual Revolution* (1945), and an Austrian psychoanalyst influenced by Freud, rejected Freud's negative version of restraint. Instead of presenting the positive version that depends on receptivity, Reich simply rejected restraint. The cultural shift from the compulsive to the impulsive character, from the puritan to the playboy, was then inevitable.

Playboy magazine first appeared in 1953, a half century after Sigmund Freud's first publication. This purveyor of recreational sex began as an explicit reaction against puritan moralism and Victorian prudishness. The magazine's philosophy bolted with a vengeance to the opposite extreme. The performance drive of the compulsive character gave way to the performance drive of the impulsive character. Puritan sublimation of sexual impulses and Victorian repression of sexual feelings gave way to impulsive expression, and an unhealthy preoccupation with performance techniques.

From Spiritual Helplessness to Sexual Helplessness ("What can you do about sex?")

Beneath the performance drive of the puritan was his spiritual helplessness—"I can do nothing about my salvation." Underlying the performance drive of the playboy is his sexual helplessness—"I can do nothing about my sexual impulses; I have to express them or else get sick. And while I'm at it I might as well get out of it everything I can."

When the warmth and intimacy of God was lost in Calvinism, and people felt evil and impotent in the void, the response became, "If I cannot get involved in my spiritual salvation, I can get involved in controlling my impulses to prove that I am one of the saved." Moralism became the "I can do it" reaction against spiritual helplessness.

Then, when the playboy reacted against moralism, he abandoned himself to his sexual urges with the idea that all control is unhealthy. He falsely assumed that if too much control can be so bad, then no control at all must be much better.

Subconsciously, however, the playboy reacted against his inability (helplessness) to do anything about controlling his impulses. His self-proving reaction became the "I can do it" of sexual performance. The spiritual helplessness of the puritan eventually became the sexual helplessness of the playboy in spite of the latter's performance-virtuosity and skill.

Ordinarily, we do not associate the playboy with sexual impotence, the usual meaning of which is genital incompetence. But sexuality means much more than genital sex. It is the total energy of manhood and womanhood, and includes the power to control sexual impulses.

Since a man is a man, and a woman is a woman, in their entire selves, not just in their genital organs, sexual competence involves the wholeness of manhood and womanhood. Sexual potency involves the ability to integrate genital sex into unconditional love and into emotional intimacy between a man and a woman. When this ability is impaired by impulsiveness and performance-for-its-own-sake, the individual is sexually, if not yet genitally, paralyzed.

Sexual dysfunction in the area of emotional intimacy and commitment tends to affect genital competence. For example, one promiscuous young man reported on a national television interview that he was impotent when he eventually got married. He discovered that he was emotionally unable to integrate sex with love and commitment.

63

Frequent sex without loving commitment might be genitally functional, but it is sexually inadequate. When tenderness, patience, and sacrifice are avoided because they get in the way of lust for pleasure and power, at least ninety percent of human sexual energy is put out of action. The result can be coolness and even cunning, often in the guise of a captivating charm.

Emotions are mysterious and elusive. Sharing them is full of risk and self-giving. When feelings include hurt, loneliness, fear, uncertainty, and sadness, most playboys, because they lack deep receptivity, decide they will have nothing to do with emotions. Having a good time is their first priority.

It is just as easy to short-circuit one's emotional life by concentrating on sexual performance as on work performance. But such hyperactivities, though they might be effective in themselves, are largely dysfunctional. *An inability to relate performance with intimacy and with loving commitment is the common source of both spiritual and sexual helplessness*.

Efficiency in performance of any kind is a masculine quality. Emotional intimacy is a more feminine quality.

Intimacy is the natural and necessary context for efficiency. Relationships are the environment and basic reason for occupations and achievements. Work without love for someone is a raw masculine endeavor unintegrated with the feminine side of life. In spite of its efficiency, it is essentially powerless.

The *affective* side of life is meant to be the source of strength and energy for the *effective* side of life.[7] Unless we *are moved* or inspired in our hearts, we cannot *move* outward toward a goal with an authentic capacity for action. We are like a sailboat that cannot receive the wind and has to be rowed, instead of one that moves with lifted sails.

Receptivity is the origin of potency. Involvement of the heart is the true source of power in both religious and sexual activity.

From Fear of Condemnation
to Fear of Repression

Reacting against puritanism, the playboy rightly denies the puritan idea that human nature is totally depraved by sin. But he fails to see the difference between depravity and deprivation. His failure to discern the difference leads him into the opposite wrong assumption from that of the puritan.

Though we are not depraved by our alienation from God and from ourselves and others (sin), we are deeply deprived. Failing to recognize this truth between the extremes of total evil and total goodness, the playboy can see himself only in the latter extreme: almost total (or sinless) goodness.

Subconsciously, however, the playboy is as negative as the puritan toward human nature. He fears the mysterious capacity of his inner self for repressing the sex drive. This fear makes him want to prove he is not repressing a single sexual feeling. As a result, he becomes impulsive.

The contemporary American fears repression as much as the puritan feared condemnation. Both objects of fear are hidden in the unconscious mind. Both kinds of fear are, at bottom, a misunderstanding of, and anxiety about, the feminine.

If the playboy really understood the receptive side of himself, he could receive his sexual feelings consciously, instead of unconsciously repressing them, or fearing repression. But since he closes off the intimate, receptive side of himself, he puts himself in his own predicament.

The rejected feminine side of the spiritual life caused the puritan to fear condemnation; the same denial of the feminine causes the playboy to fear repression. Liberation of the feminine within the person is the answer to both fears.

The puritan reacted to his fear of condemnation by trying to prove he was one of God's elite. The playboy reacts to his fear of repression by trying to prove he is not repressing, and that he is, indeed, one of the sexual elite.

Fear of condemnation caused the puritan's negative restraint of feelings, which, as we have seen, grew into the Victorian's repression of feelings. The playboy's subsequent reaction against this negative restraint and repression, and his neurotic fear of repression, are clearly traceable, by the very nature of the reaction, to the puritan's fear of condemnation.

Though the playboy and the puritan have different ways of escaping their anxiety, one in sex and the other in work, both are anxious about something *out of control* in themselves. Both are uneasy about the repressed feminine side within them. And both take flight from anxiety into achievement.

From Individualism to Selfism

The puritan was an individualist concerned about building character through a masculine kind of reason and willpower. He did what he thought he should no matter how he felt, and no matter what other people were feeling, thinking, and doing.

The contemporary style of individualist, the selfist, has the opposite characteristics. He (she too) is concerned about feeling good, and feeling guiltless, no matter what he does, and is very interested in what others feel, think, and do. The selfist does not care, however, what other people consider right and wrong, or moral and immoral; that is irrelevant and just "too personal."

Strong on wants and weak on responsibility, the selfist claims rights without duties, and demands to have needs and wants satisfied immediately. This impulsive type of character looks for a self-fulfilling career, and demands the freedom to develop one's own potential. Change and mobility are seen as necessary for these purposes. Commitment is avoided because it "ties you down" and "closes you off."

Strangely, however, the quest for fulfillment is not always fulfilling. Emptiness haunts the edges, then the deeper levels, of life.

Seeking your own identity can result in losing your identity. True self-identity requires stability and roots. Moving from one place to another, changing careers, divorcing, remarrying, and divorcing again, is uprooting. When you do not know who you are in your stable (not static) foundation, your ability to relate with another person is diminished. Your capacity for intimacy is impaired.

In a culture where the medium is the message, where manner is more important than substance, where lifestyles replace life commitments, and where careers tend to replace vocations, the being of the self is often dissipated. A lifestyle is not one's substance and identity. A career is not necessarily a commitment to love someone else.

Seeing these essential differences between style and substance, William Kilpatrick said, "The present era has been variously described as the age of liberation, the age of transformation, even the age of a new consciousness. At some future date, however, we may look back and discover that it was, in reality, the age during which we lost our identity, and with it, our ability to love." [8]

Intimacy reveals the worst as well as the best in people. Unless we can cherish another person in their dark side as well as in their goodness, we cannot love that person. When we want only the pleasant and the fulfilling, when we repress the pain of our own faults and refuse to admit our own guilt, we cannot bear the faults and weaknesses of another. We are afraid of their faults, and do not want to be disillusioned by them. This fear makes us distance the other person, thus frustrating our own need to give and receive love. We build for ourselves a house of narcissism: solitary confinement in our own feelings and impulses. The anxiety of loneliness is inevitable.[9]

From Parent to Child

The puritan family was strong and disciplined. But it contained the elements of its own eventual breakdown. In the latter part of the 20th century, when children became economic liabilities rather than assets, puritan family motivations became severely strained.

In the age of production, children were producers. They were wanted because of the work they could do on the farm or in the family's business. They were desired for their economic value. They possessed a clear social identity.

But when producers divided into employers and employees, much of the world of work was separated from the domestic scene and relocated in factories. Eventually, child labor ended, and children became non-productive consumers. Education became more complex, longer, and more expensive. Delayed adulthood meant a longer parental responsibility for offspring. Parents became confused as to why they wanted children.

At the same time, children became confused as to why they existed. Conditioned by the continuing prevalence of the work-ethic, and without some kind of identity in work, they could not feel needed by their parents. Often they felt useless and helpless. When women began leaving home to go to work in factories and offices, the emotional vacuum deepened.

In the meantime, the non-producing, consuming young people continued to develop physically and sexually. Since they could not sublimate their sex drive into work as much as they formerly did, they became more interested in sex as such. This situation encouraged the young to question the strict moral code of their parents. Sexual indulgence, drug abuse, and juvenile crime increased. The playboy culture emerged, not only out of the childhood of the new age, but also out of the child and adolescent spirit in many adults who had rebelled against puritanism.

The Child Rejects the Parent

The playboy character was begotten by the puritan character; not by the will of the parent figure, but rather by a revolt within the offspring himself. The puritan son became a playboy when he turned against both the feminine and masculine deficiencies in puritanism.

The playboy type of character reacted against the absence of the feminine—unconditional love and affirming care of feelings—by denying the value of these qualities. Then, in order to do whatever he desired without restraint, he turned against the overbearing masculine qualities of puritanism, its moralistic and industrious values. "Do as you choose and have fun doing it" became his cry of liberation.

Unwittingly, however, the playboy remained the puritan's begotten. His attack on puritan moralism, instead of freeing him from puritanism, only embedded him more deeply in its pathology.

The playboy is no less compulsive and moralistic about his own self-proving ethic. He, too, is driven to perform. And he, too, is self-righteous about the absolute value of his particular skills. For him, sexual performance unhindered by love, commitment, and care for feelings is like a new kind of religion.

Though the playboy and puritan seem basically different at first glance, a closer look shows that the playboy's reaction took place within the puritan's perspective. The rejecting child, though seeming to escape the influence of his forebears, actually remained in the same cultural "house" with them. Playboyism, in an inverted way, is a form of puritanism.

In conclusion, we have seen the swinging between extremes that happens in the masculine side of human nature and culture when the feminine side is repressed. Our culture is now in danger of swinging away from its playboy character back into something like the original puritan character, then back again to its opposite, unless the feminine power for integrating opposites emerges. More receptivity in the spontaneous and responsible parts of the self could unite and balance them, and could stop the futile swinging of the historical pendulum.

Before this happens, however, women will have to wake up and make a difference. The women's movement will have to recognize the puritan and playboy mentalities within itself. Women will have to look more closely, especially, at the contemporary playboy mentality, and see how this presence in the air they breathe is destroying them while promising a better quality of life.

CHAPTER SIX

THE IMPOTENT PLAYBOY

The playboy is a cultural character more than he is any individual person. "He" is a penetrating presence, a spirit of the times, a controlling image and script in the minds of many.

Most American men today do not consider themselves playboys. But the playboy version of the puritan mentality is influencing everyone in different ways and degrees. The playboy image, a stereotype that fits no one in particular, has been, nevertheless, a powerful force in shaping the self-concept of blue-collar as well as white-collar males.

Millions of Americans, both men and women, have been affected by the compliant playmate who presents no question about emotional and spiritual bonding, and by the sophisticated male attitude that would tolerate no such threat. The playboy mentality has become part of our national character.

We hear the voice of this mentality everywhere in the media and in the way people ordinarily talk. "Do whatever you choose." "Follow your own preferences." "There is no connection between sex and marriage unless you choose to connect them." "There is no connection between sex and babies unless you want a baby." These are some of the mentality's favorite lines.

According to the attitude and the image, loving commitment would disturb the playboy's equilibrium. Frequency and efficiency below the waistline comprise his center of interest. Around this center he uses personality as a stimulant. His own and his partner's personhood are outside the scope of attention. Beyond the horizon of recreational sex (a kind of sport) too many confusing complexities introduce themselves. So these are suavely ignored as irrelevant.

The higher his degree of sophistication, the more the playboy invests in recreational foreplay: skiing, swimming, sailing, horseback riding, gourmet dining....But all variations of this strategic finesse are calculated with a single aim in view. All roads lead to bed.

Though he is a dedicated sexual activist, the playboy has a largely inactive sexuality. He fails to realize that he is sexual in all of himself, not just in the bedroom-oriented part of himself.

People are not like centaurs; they are not composed of sexed bodies with sexless minds attached. Instead, the body and the person are one. And the person is much more than the body.

When a man thinks and acts like a playboy, the sexuality of his mind descends from the power of unconditional love and commitment to the powerlessness of impulses that lack the passion of great meanings and values. His main sexual organ, his brain, deflates from its full sexual capacity to its erotic dimension. Sex then loses its wholeness and its natural orientation. Every kind of sexual disorientation, which he cunningly calls an orientation, begins to surface. Each is redefined as normal and moral. Anyone inclined to think differently is regarded as a fossil of the puritan era.

At a certain point of saturation, playboy attitudes and maxims become cultural scripts that generate a new cultural character. Sexual preference becomes the dominant standard of behavior. Yet sex itself is not considered a preference, but an obligation. Only the style of expression is a matter of choice. Those who do not participate, or who fail, in the sex game are regarded as aberrations.

As the new culture's preference-imperatives replace the previous culture's moralistic imperatives, the impulsive part of the self buries alive the responsible part of the self. Any mention of self-control, surfacing like a choked whisper from bygone times, is promptly dissipated by calling it "unhealthy" or "immoral."

The male who is vulnerable to such influences tends to become casual in his attitude toward sex. As he becomes an increasingly more accomplished connoisseur of recreational relationships, his sexual emotions recede and often disappear. He becomes emotionally detached and flaccid. His sexual capacity for feelings in the heart and commitment in the will becomes devitalized. In the midst of intense, effective sexplay his trans-genital sexual powers remain limp. Behind his charming personality no one is present. Nobody is home. The playboy is sexually, if not yet genitally, paralyzed.

But genital incompetence, the final embarrassment, often ensues. Thousands of American males are now going to therapists complaining about sexual (genital) dysfunction. Though this problem can have various physical and psychological causes, an energy-disturbance in the main sexual organ, or in the male's philosophy of life, is rarely recognized as a cause.

His Kind of Choice

When the sexual powers of the mind and soul are put out of action, sexual perceptions and decisions become distorted. Values are then based on reflexes and urges, not on inner requirements for human wholeness. "Do whatever you choose" becomes the emasculated masculine guide for action.

Life is viewed as a kind of supermarket. You choose whatever packaging, taste or style you like. The more choices you have the freer you are thought to become. The substance of what you choose has little or no significance. If you prefer sadomasochistic sex and your partner is willing, choosing this activity makes you sexually free. If, however, you do not prefer such activity, you remain free by choosing not to choose it. You do not have to buy everything in the supermarket.

73

An impulsive shopper does not realize that the content of his or her choices has more to do with freedom than having a choice and the number of options available. What looks attractive and tastes good might be toxic with additives or nutritionally depleted. The effect on health could undermine the individual's other options.

A supermarket rendition of freedom of choice is the playboy's version of puritan willpower.

To the advocate of willpower, compulsive goals and duties are all that matter. "Feelings don't count!" By sheer force of will, the individual follows these compulsions simply to perform well and to prove he is one of the chosen.

To the advocate of choice, on the other hand, impulses and urges are all that really matter. Feelings don't count much either, especially feelings of the heart and soul. And even those physical feelings and psychological preferences that do seem to matter are not received reflectively before they are expressed. The individual follows his impulses to prove to himself and everyone else that he is really liberated and free.

Both the "choice" and the "willpower" versions of freedom are unhealthy. True freedom unites impulses with will, and preference with principle, in the whole good of life. The integrating factor is the receptive (pondering in the heart), feminine side of the soul.

When we receive our feelings into our affirming awareness, we realize we do not have to act on all of our feelings and their impulses. Then we become really free. We can choose to act or not to act. We also realize that we need to take care of our feelings by expressing them wisely and according to natural principles of integrity. By receiving both our feelings and our principles together, we become authentically free.

His Pathological Sophistication

Sophistication is usually associated with worldly wisdom and learning. It can be a good thing to have, but only if it does not make people mentally aloof and emotionally cool. When used to distance and put down reality, and when this distancing becomes a habitual attitude, sophistication becomes a pathological condition or a disease. The sophisticate is an individual with an extremely "above it all" attitude.

The playboy sophisticate is usually far removed from such a "low brow" matter as sexual morality. He is able to rationalize his sexual incompetence until it seems a most reasonable and convincing perfection. He believes he is well-informed and fully grownup. He becomes a highly eloquent, articulate, and accomplished philosopher of impulse-consumption. He is adept at using grownup terms to justify arrested, or childish, behavior. With a kind of peerless mental alchemy, he defends each disorientation as part of the creative repertoire of the sexually liberated. Even bestiality comes under the sophisticated expression "sexual preference." And abortion is whitewashed by phrases like "termination of pregnancy" or "removal of pregnancy tissue" or a "medical procedure."

The playboy sophisticate finds the intuitions of the "peasant" intolerable. He spurns "grassroots instinct" as unpolished and embarrassingly emotional. Such an attitude is found in many of the society's professionals and experts.

For example, Dr. C.V., a gynecologist, testified in his state legislature about the complications of second trimester abortions. He presented an elaborate, detached description of the "procedure" he uses. He explained how he performs a dilatation and curretage, how he cuts the fetal tissue into pieces and removes the separated parts, then reassembles them to make sure all have been removed.

After he finished his scientifically presented testimony, one of the legislators on the hearing committee groaned aloud, "I'm glad I'm not one of those unborn babies." On his way out of the room, Dr. C.V. lost his sophistication as he remarked to a sympathetic bystander, "I wonder where that simpleton comes from. The place probably doesn't even have a zipcode."

The more "educated" he is, the more likely the playboy is a sophisticate. The underlying cause of his disoriented thinking, however, is not so much a lack of intellectual ability as sexual incompetence. He thinks this condition is smart, cool, and suave because it is liberated from what he regards as antiquated, obsolete, traditions.

His Anti-Fertility Attitude

One of the most archaic of all traditions, according to the sophisticate's point of view, is respect for human fertility. The up-to-date and "with it" idea is that you can do with your fertility whatever you choose, as far as technology facilitates your choices. Whatever an extremely masculinized (imposed control) technology can prevent, and whatever it can bring about, is "where the action is." Concern for natural, "merely biological," processes is due only to the ignorance and emotionalism of "peasants."

The playboy's attitude toward his normal, natural fertility reveals a great deal about his sexual adequacy. If he thinks he and the female are able to produce in her uterus a "clump of cells," or "a mass of protoplasm," or "products of conception," or a "sex-induced tumor," his view of his own sexual potency is thereby debilitated. *It takes much less sexual potency to start the growth of a clump of cells than to begin the life of another human person.*

The male who can look upon the destroyed life of his aborted child and say, "I can do nothing about that," admits his sexual helplessness. Though he might be a dazzling bedroom performer, he is impotent as a man. Ironically, he is sure to imagine himself to be at the height of his sexual potency.

The woman who wants to "control her body" by knowing her body (in her fertility cycles) and by expecting the male's cooperation with this knowledge, is an unnerving threat to the playboy. Unless he persuades her to adopt his way of thinking, she regards her fertility as a normal and healthy part of her entire personhood.

But he thinks her fertility is a kind of disease. He thinks their shared fertility is just a part of their animal biology. And he often chooses to get himself fixed, similar to his treatment of his household pet.

Likewise, thinking that the fertility of persons is a merely biological matter or a female disturbance, playboy-influenced physicians feel impelled either to medicate or surgically to "correct" the fertility of the female, often pitied as "the poor thing." At the same time, these physicians get rich from the normal, natural "disease" in women's bodies.

Those males who, for the profit-value of the procedure, remove "fetal parts" from women's bodies, and reassemble these parts to make sure the uterus is cleaned out, are able to do so only because of hardness, sadism, and sexual deformity. Unless the playboy culture can thus clean up after itself (while women pay the price), the playboy cannot so easily persuade the female to be his playmate.

His Frigid Playmate

The playmate is the female who lets the playboy do her thinking for her while she "knows" she is doing her own thinking for herself. She champions his version of choice. She takes on his pathological sophistication. She lives by his anti-fertility attitude. She is his extension. He is her perspective.

Many cultures have treated women as men's property, as mothers of men's children, as servers of men's needs and desires. Today, a male-developed technology performs many of the tasks formerly done by women. The freed female has time to become a partner in the playboy's preoccupations. But she is still his. His machines, gadgets, and devices have liberated her from being *his* servant to becoming *his* playmate.

Because she wants his approval and attention, the playmate adjusts to the playboy's expectations. She cannot imagine herself existing without male attentions. So she plays *his* game. She does whatever it takes to please him. She fits herself into his disorientations and dysfunctions. She instinctively feels that if she began to challenge his sophisticated ideology, and think on her own, the playboy would simply look for another playmate.

Even the so-called "liberated" woman adjusts herself into the male frame of reference. She moves around in a man's world with assertiveness and even aggression, and competes with men for the highest managerial and executive positions. She becomes the male's workmate.

Many of these same women want also to be playmates. They get into the male's game as well as his version of work. His male philosophy of sex grows on them along with his male philosophy of commercialism. They are certain they have just as much right to sex without strings attached as do the males. They, too, set out on the road of sex by preference and choice.

The "liberated" playmate has learned that she is multi-orgasmic and has a greater capacity for this response than males. Some females have concluded that it might be more reasonable for them to have several partners at the same time in their life, so they will be able to satisfy their capacity. They are not concerned about the other energies of their sexuality that will go unsatisfied. Since these other energies are ignored, this style of female is already deeply into sexual frigidity, even though she believes she is highly responsive.

There are two basic kinds of playmate: the kitten that purrs for sex and the cat that prowls. The cat is a reaction against the condition of the kitten, and grows out of the kitten. The cat sometimes becomes a tigress and even a lioness.

Such animal designations aptly signify the playmate's adjustment to the biological fixations of the playboy.

The kitten inflates her physical assets. She turns on the exciting side of her personality and masks other sides of herself that might turn off the playboy's interest. Her energies are focused on encouraging the male's advances.

The cat, on the other hand, refuses to fit herself into the "merely physical" ideals of the playboy. Instead of *adjusting* to him, she *identifies* with him. She wants to enjoy his prerogatives, especially sexual independence. She does not want to encourage male advances; she can make advances of her own. She insists that the only real difference between women and men is their "reproductive anatomy," and that this difference can be neutralized rather easily with technology.

Females who resent the deep responsiveness that is woman's emphasis often dedicate themselves to a psychological neutering of persons, a sexless interpretation of women and men beyond their anatomy. This is the female sophisticate's kind of sexual frigidity; it is motivated by fear of her deeper sexuality and womanhood.

In the hypnotic spell of the playboy culture, neither men nor women can imagine a lasting male-female relationship between two sexually attractive people that does not go, eventually, to bed. Genital gravitation goes unquestioned. No playmate, whether kitten or cat, would dare to question it. Any playboy would rush to stamp out the tiny flame of a possible insight.

The playmate believes, along with the playboy, that sexual activity means little more than pelvic activity. Sexual emotions are thought to be wired in one way only—for arousal. This serious limitation of the male and female potential in human beings is the crippling source of sexual—not necessarily genital—dysfunction.

Since the body and the person are an integral whole, a woman's perception of her body and its sexual functions is also her perception of herself as a person.

In her conscious mind, a woman might feel convinced that she is whole and healthy, while she treats her normal, natural cycles of fertility as an enemy of her freedom. But her subconscious mind is not fooled.

79

In her deeper self she needs to be sexually responsive to her own generative power. Otherwise she might frigidly reject it. She needs to *receive* her fertility into her self-awareness. She needs to regulate her fertility through self-knowledge instead of prostituting herself to male-devised appliances, medications, and surgeries.

Before she can do this, however, she needs to discover the power of her own mind to know her own body. And she needs to become assertive enough to expect the male to cooperate with her appreciation of her fertility.

The female whose body-concept is formed by the playboy culture, but who imagines she is controlling her own body, is being controlled instead by playboy sophistications. By availing herself of his neutralizing devices, she thinks she is controlling her own body. She is unaware that the playboy culture, by controlling her mind and her concept of her body, is actually controlling her body for her. She is the one who gets vacuumed out after sex, not the playboy. And the playboy is pleased to have it that way.

As male physicians remove male-induced "growths" from her female organs, she parrots scripts that gratify playboy ears. She sounds knowledgeable, scientific, realistic, and chic in what she says about "reproductive freedom." She is, however, unaware of the puritan and playboy origins of her "wanting and unwanting" point of view.

A sexually whole and vital woman knows that she has the power to conceive another of her kind—another human person, however small and undeveloped at first. She might live in a slum, but her self-concept as a woman is rich.

Another woman living in an upper-class suburb might think she is capable of conceiving a mass of protoplasmic tissue, or a sex-induced "growth," or a potential human being at most. In spite of her economic wealth, her self-concept as a woman is severely deprived.

The female who prostitutes herself to "the procedure" that removes the "products of conception" or "fetal material" seals off the core of her womanhood with mental contrivances. If she can

80

look upon the destroyed body of her aborted child and say, "This is my right to privacy," she might be multi-orgasmic, but she is frigid as a woman.

While the male chauvinist playboy judges the female as wanted or unwanted, the female chauvinist playmate judges her child as wanted or unwanted. She has learned well from the playboy. Her response to her unwanted child fails to give the playboy the example he needs to treat *her* any differently. She endorses and solidifies his stance. And she calls this *her* freedom to choose.

CHAPTER SEVEN

HE SEDUCES A NATION

As the masculine mentality, the "he" of the American character, changed from its puritan to its playboy phase, the sexual revolution gained momentum. By the mid 1960s, the playboy reaction against puritan moralism boosted the revolution into national prominence. Since then, "do as you choose" attitudes have been spreading throughout the society and its institutions.

In a wave of conservatism, however, a reaction against the playboy culture has now begun. Will we change our national character into something more balanced and mature by bringing in the feminine side of the mind? Or will we just move back into another form of the original puritanism?

In order to answer with a balanced awareness, we need to see what the new conservatism is reacting against. If the object of the reaction is an extreme condition, we can take note of its contrary pole or antithesis, and decide to avoid that extreme. We can look for the integrating center between the extremes that would help to give balance and maturity to the American character.

The new conservatism is reacting against the consequences of impulsive choice. None of these consequences have strengthened our society. They have weakened it instead. Unmarried sex and pregnancy, adultery, child abuse, "raw sewage" pornography, venereal disease including herpes and

AIDS, drug abuse and alcoholism (among other things) have mushroomed on the scene like a nuclear cloud.

A reaction against this flood of symptoms is in order. But an attack on symptoms is a crisis-measure that can produce another, and equally devastating, problem. The real answer is to treat the cause of the symptoms.

The cause is a disorder within us, a bad relationship between the spontaneous and responsible parts of ourselves. At the heart of this ailing connection is an absence of receptivity in the responsible part of ourselves. This receptivity is the connecting element. It is the integrating power that can change a bad inner relationship into a good one.

Without the receptive power, the spontaneous part of ourselves becomes impulsive, and the responsible part becomes compulsive. Then we are vulnerable to impulsive or compulsive figures and scripts in the world around us. Some of us are more pliable than others. Some are more easily seduced. When enough of us get taken in, our general culture assumes the character of most of its participants.

Like an unhealthy child coming from an unhealthy parent, the playboy mentality is coming from the absence of receptivity in the responsible part of ourselves. This absence (unreceived or ignored feelings) is causing the spontaneous part of ourselves to become impulsive. It is causing many of us to lose our substantial selves in a way that makes us look for the support of our peers. "Everybody is doing it" becomes our culture's cry of self-righteousness.

An impulsive culture that promotes freedom of choice without restraint, naturally becomes voracious with desires. Consumerism flourishes. Profits become more important than substance. A stepped-up appetite for things and experiences depletes natural resources, not only in the environment, but also in the self. All kinds of waste matter, in huge quantities, pollute the physical and social surroundings, and consciousness itself.

At the same time, impulsive behavior, protected by psychology, disrupts the family, and undermines social and religious authority. Emotional problems are blamed on parents, society, and religion, not on the real cause within the self. Everyone else is to blame, not me. I'm innocent, OK, sin-free, and guiltless.

No Sin Except Guilt

Proponents of the playboy culture acknowledge no sexual sin except guilt about sex. They moralize against guilt as solemnly as the puritans moralized against sin. The repression of honest guilt (not the same as neurotic guilt) then makes the culture casual and cool about sex.

As psychologist Rollo May has pointed out, a woman used to feel guilty if she said yes; now she feels guilty if she says no. Even the "liberated" female feels sinful when she disobeys the sex-imperatives of the playboy culture. Refusal to perform, or inability to perform, are the only failures for which guilt is excusable.

When the spontaneous part of life rejects the responsible part and becomes impulsive, people tend to think that sex exists only for fun, and that this fun is completely innocent and sinless no matter what the situation. Because guilt defiles the absolute purity of fun-sex, the only sexual sin is thought to be guilt. Such an assertion is destined to seep into many unbalanced minds, and to stimulate an inclination toward rape, sexual abuse of children, and other forms of sexual abuse.

Ironically, the ideology of guilt-free sex, while it could be a stimulant for rape, denies a connection between rape and sex, and defines rape, instead, as violence. Sex appears so innocent that rape is said by many to have no connection with sex.

While rape is basically a matter of violence, the connection between sex and violence must not be overlooked. Whenever sex is isolated from loving commitment between a man and woman, it naturally tends to connect with violence. Rape is a problem of unintegrated sex, as well as a problem of brutal aggression.

84

Impulsive sex, especially when it becomes habitual and ideologically OK, is not designed to hold its place for long. It often leads to hurt, anger, depression, and suicide. It leaves people strangely joyless, helpless, and desperate. They start demanding in a childish way that their needs be met by others, including the parent-substitute, the government. They feel guilty for not always having a good time, or for feeling sad. When authentic guilt is buried alive, it "breaks out around the edges" in many variations of distress.

The Effect on Young People

Swept along on the waves of the sexual revolution, many young people have made "sex whenever you feel like it" their standard of behavior. Following the standard eventually makes sex boring. To keep it interesting, partners become disposable. "Everyone is doing it" makes sex a duty, even if it gets tedious. So you do it even when you don't feel like it. The original "feel like it" standard has a strange way of undoing itself.

The "other-directed" pressure of peers is no less constricting than the "inner-directed" pressure of moralism. Teens become pregnant, not always because they desire to have sex, but because sex is simply the thing to do. And the push is as strong, sometimes stronger, from young female peers as from the males.

The presence of playboy helplessness about sex appears in the attitude of adults toward the young. "You're going to do it anyway, so learn to protect yourself against the consequences."

Along with this sexual helplessness (a passivity that results from a lack of true inner receptivity), a neurotic fear of guilt causes sex educators to separate facts about biology from emotional and moral values. Instead of reducing incidents of unmarried pregnancy, venereal disease, and other kinds of teen trauma, such a split education fosters more of every kind of distress. Considering the results, this type of sex education reveals itself as a sophisticated form of child abuse.

85

Social agencies acting as parent substitutes treat problems such as pregnancy and venereal disease as if their cause, a culture of impulsiveness, did not exist. Merely to mention, or to hint at, a moral connection between these problems and sex is wholly unacceptable because it might produce anxiety and guilt. And these conditions are thought to be much more harmful than unplanned pregnancy or venereal disease.

Anyone who would dare to risk the perpetration of a guilt feeling in a young person with sex problems would be commiting the worst kind of sin. He or she would be stepping backward into puritanism. Suggesting guilt with regard to sexual behavior cannot be allowed by the playboy culture, not even in a slip of the tongue.

While moralizing to young people is not the answer, some positive and encouraging education about the natural connection of sex with the family is a more holistic treatment of the problem.

When a culture represses the natural bonding of sex with a loving life-commitment, the natural relation of sex with fertility becomes unclear. Many teens, when they suddenly find themselves pregnant, react as if they had no idea how such a thing could happen to them.

By their shocked response they seem to say, "I didn't know there is a connection between sex and babies. I thought sex is for fun; that's what everyone says it's for."

The sex-educated young of today appear to know as little about the cause of pregnancy as the young of the Victorian era when sex was barely mentioned by anyone. Since blatant sex and buried sex are both repressive, though differently, they are equally sources of ignorance and frustration.

The Parent Rejects the Child

Without a receptive awareness of both feelings and values, it is not possible to unite opposites like spontaneity and restraint.

But this unity of opposites is necessary for every kind of human wholeness; it is important to all the human arts.

Figure skating, for example, requires both spontaneity and discipline. So does driving a car and cooking a meal. So does the general art of living.

A civilization almost totally formed by a male mentality lacks the receptive ability to unite spontaneity and restraint. It also lacks, for the same reason, the ability to unite child and parent. The parent becomes compulsive instead of restraining in a healthy way. And the child becomes impulsive instead of spontaneous in a healthy way. The result is a broken inner character, and a disintegration in the parent-child relationship.

We have seen how the parental character of the puritan begot the childish character of the playboy. As the impulsive progeny of puritanism became parents themselves, they were not destined to have a healthy sense of the child or of parenthood. Often they rejected, and now reject, their own children. The culture of the *unhealthy child* is also the culture of the *unwanted child*.

Unwanted children always existed in the past. But in the playboy era, the unwanted child is an accepted matter of sheer preference.

In the past, the expression "unwanted child" was meant as a judgment on the lack of love in the parent; now it is a judgment on the child. Children are regarded merely as desirable or undesirable *objects*, similar to things. They are not valued as good in themselves, *any more than the puritan God valued his children as good in themselves*. The children of choice-minded parents are the main commodity and waste product of the playboy's sexual revolution.

CHAPTER EIGHT

HIS IMPOTENCE PEAKS

As the playboy mentality emerged in the communications media, "wanted and unwanted" scripts surged around the practice of contraception. "If you do not want a baby, take the pill or insert a diaphragm." Even temporary abstinence in marriage became quite unthinkable; it was called, by some, a mutilation.

At first, abortion was rarely mentioned. But the result of contraceptive failures was not destined to be welcomed with open arms. Pressures to legalize abortion began almost immediately.

Abortion, however, was not as easily accepted as contraception. It met with more resistance in the grassroots population and the legislatures. So the spirit of the sexual revolution, through some of its advocates, was forced to turn to the Courts. This spirit and its advocates had to persuade at least five of the nine Supreme Court Justices to search the farthest reaches of the Constitution and to find in it the playboy agenda.

As feminist cries to "control my own body" soared in the media and rattled the rafters of the republic, the supreme law of the land was forced to yield the desired results. The playboy mentality "pulling the strings behind the scene" was urging the tigress to growl and the lioness to roar. The masculine spirit of the times dearly hoped that the feminists would succeed.

After all, a Constitution formed by puritans and deists did not imply, even in its darkest shadows, that sex could be a free-for-all matter. There was no evidence that any political thinker of the 18th century thought that a Constitution should deal with sex. Furthermore, the puritans were opposed to abortion.

But the playboy had to get his playmate and "her" freedom of choice firmly installed in Constitutional interpretation, otherwise he could not be fully, freely, and legally himself. Somewhere, somehow, some women had to get the message and take a case to Court.

A case in Court ultimately faces the Constitution. Could an appeal for the abortion-choice pass the supreme test?

About the Constitution

The individualism of the Western world reached its height in the revolutionary Constitution of the United States of America written by the Constitutional Congress of 1787. This framework of government was designed for a democratic republic by a group of white, Protestant males for the protection of their interests. The interests of native Americans, blacks, women, and children were not *explicitly* protected by the original Constitution. This lack of clearly stated protection did not mean, however, that the interests of these people were excluded. At times the Courts excluded them. But these judicial errors were corrected by constitutional amendments subsequently enacted by the people.

The Declaration of Independence of 1776 (a philosophy of government) and the Constitution (a framework of government) based government on the natural rights of individuals. When, as in other forms of government, rights are given either by a monarch or by a State, the individual is treated as a child in relation to a parent. But when rights are recognized in the God-created nature of the individual, the State is founded to protect these natural rights, not to give or to take them away at will. According to the Declaration, "We hold these truths to be self-evident, that all men are created equal, that they are endowed by their Creator with certain unalienable rights, that among these are Life, Liberty and the pursuit of Happiness."

A democratic government based on laws that protect natural rights is a great advancement in human history. Its principles of self-regulation (government by the people) are able to unite opposites such as liberty and law. It is also able to balance the legislative, executive, and judicial powers of government. The balance, however, is tenuous and easy to lose. One or more of the three powers can become too strong.

Because the Supreme Court judges are not elected by the people, but are appointed for life, this branch of government is the least subject to checks and balances, and marks a weak spot in the system. Cultural pressures easily creep into Constitutional interpretation. The Justices can then slip into *making* law instead of *interpreting* law, thus encroaching on the law-making or legislative power of government. The need for wisdom in the interpreters is imperative.

The so-called "right to privacy," because it requires a wise distinction between the public and private realms, has become a special danger zone for the intrusion of legislating judges. The wisdom required to avoid such an intrusion involves an understanding of the human being *as a person*, not just as an individual. A culture so strongly grounded in individualism as our own tends to lack some of this required wisdom.

According to the mentality of the framers, the Constitution presupposed a clear distinction between public and private life, and was especially concerned to govern *public* affairs. Nothing was said about privacy. No mention was made of the family, because the family was viewed as belonging to the *private* realm. No mention was made of women in the original Constitution, because women, too, were viewed as belonging within the private realm of the family. As an individualist, the father belonged to the public realm and was the legal representative for the family. He was a family man mainly in private. By protecting the interests of the individualist, private as well as public, the Constitution indirectly protected the family.

Developed in the context of puritanism and the Enlightenment, the Constitution of the United States is an agreement between individualists, and is not based on a concept of society as a family. Previously, society was seen as a kind of extended family. The family had a public as well as a private dimension. A monarchy was a public family. The massive religious move from the family to the individual (from the "papa" who interpreted the Bible for the family, to the individual who did this for himself) may have done more than anything in history to shift the basis of society from the family to the individual.

The same puritan who moved interpretation of the Bible from a public authority into the privacy of individual conscience eventually abandoned government by kings and moved the family from the public to the private sphere of life. The abandoned interpreting authority for the Bible crept in the back door, however, when the framers established an interpreting authority for the Constitution. And the abandoned rule by kings crept in, hiddenly, along with it. How to prevent the interpreters from acting like a monarchy is a problem built into the system. Ironically, the feared monarchical impulse eventually showed up, as we shall see later, in the Supreme Court's handling of privacy and the family.

John Locke, an English philosopher who received a strict puritan upbringing, was one of the chief sources for the political theories behind both the Declaration of Independence and the Constitution. He based his thinking on the individual, not on the family.[1]

Except for the mother-infant bond, Locke saw nothing natural in the family; all the rest was mere social convention. He could not see the family as a stable basis for the social order. Much more natural to him was the self-interest of the individual. If based on private property, this self-interest would be, he thought, a stronger basis for civil law. Individual interests, not family interests, formed the "natural law" on which the "law of the land" was based.

In spite of individualistic political theory, family life based on religious and cultural traditions flourished in the private realm of

American society for almost 200 years. But when the original puritan culture began shifting into the playboy culture the effect on the family became an unprecedented jolt. Using the lever of playboy-playmate sex, the new culture catapulted women out of the private realm of the family into the "privacy" of selfists doing their own thing.

The question is not whether women should be individuals in their own right; they should. The question is whether the Constitution, under its presupposed dimension of privacy, allows for the playboy-playmate expansion of sex beyond the privacy of the family, and the resulting invasion and deterioration of the family.

The Culture and the Constitution

The Constitution of our individualist culture remains a stable frame of government while the culture moves from one phase to the next. As the culture changes, its movement inevitably affects, not the Constitution as such, but the way it is interpreted and amended.

The family versus the individual did not become a Constitutional issue until the culture developed its playboy mentality. But other issues, from the beginning of our history as a nation, dramatized the tension between the culture and the Constitution.

For example, Thomas Jefferson and others were slaveholders when they signed the Declaration proclaiming that "all men are created equal." The culture and the Declaration were at odds. Though some of these defenders of equality and liberty were uneasy with slavery, their culture did not regard the slaves as men who were created equal with themselves, but as some kind of subpersonal human organism.

In the Dred Scott decision of 1857, the federal Supreme Court ruled that black people were not legal persons, but were to be regarded as *property*. Chief Justice Roger Taney, writing the majority opinion, said that "negroes are so far inferior that they had no rights which the white man was bound to respect."

The Constitution did not support this view of black people. But the culture did. After the Civil War, the Constitution was amended (in 1865 and 1868) to recognize the human rights of black people.

Similar conflicts between the culture and the Constitution existed in relation to women and native peoples. Until 1920, women were not allowed to vote. Native Americans suffered abuse and unfair treatment from the beginning. When the puritans invited the natives to their thanksgiving feast in 1621, Governor William Bradford issued a proclamation that referred to them as "savages." [2]

On the side of the puritans, it is true that some native Americans engaged in savage acts, and that some of the puritans really cared for these original inhabitants of the continent. But it is also true that a mentality which believes that man is "an ape, a wild and savage beast," except for the elect, has a problem with human equality, even while proclaiming it.

In other words, certain cultural forces can militate against the ideal philosophy and framework of government within that culture. This same kind of conflict was destined to become more dramatic than ever when the puritan culture underwent its first major change in character.

In the 1960s, when the nation's puritan culture shifted into its playboy mode, radical changes in sexual behavior began to exert new cultural pressures on the power to interpret the Constitution. The demands of recreational sex, especially as it became dissociated from marriage and the family, certainly had no vindication in the puritan culture that previously supported the Constitution. Neither did it have any basis for endorsement in the Constitution itself. How, then, could the culture of the sexual revolution legalize the demands of family-free, fertility-free, value-free sex?

The Court in the Middle

Finding themselves in the center of the tension between puritan and playboy cultural forces, Supreme Court Justices, because they are not always wise, might side with one culture against the other, and think they are faithfully interpreting the Constitution. They might, or might not, be aware that the arbitrary rule of kings so despised by the puritans is ready, at any time, to return under cover. When that happens, the Court, under the guise of interpretation, could actually be "amending" the Constitution.

The Court is not the appointed amending body. The power of amendment belongs to the people working through the legislative branch of government. But the Justices, if they are so inclined, can usurp the legislative power of the people. What is there to stop them?

Some of the judges have admitted that they can interpret as they *want* rather than as they *should*. In his book, *The Court Years*, Justice William O. Douglas tells of the advice given him when he first became a member of the Court. Chief Justice Charles Evans Hughes told him: "Justice Douglas, you must remember one thing. At the constitutional level where we work, 90 percent of any decision is emotional. The rational part of us supplies the reasons for supporting our predilections."

After reporting this astounding admission of personal and cultural content in Court decisions, Douglas commented, "I knew judges had predilections. I knew that their moods as well as their minds were ingredients of their decisions. But I had never been willing to admit to myself that the 'gut' reaction of a judge was the main ingredient of his decision."

Justice Douglas, on the key decisions regarding the family, was to do exactly that: judge not by wisdom but by "guts," not by jurisprudence but by predilections.

In matters crucial to the harmonious functioning of the playboy culture, the Supreme Court was seduced by the culture to interpret the Constitution in steadily more novel ways. Though there was a long history of judicial revolution on other issues, the Court's "playboy" revolution had no precedent for its sheer boldness and determination to rule "from the guts." Or from the male libido.

The source of cultural pressure on the Court has not been the grassroots majority of the republic, but the loudest voices of the playboy culture: the media, articulate intellectuals, professionals, experts, and panels of experts. What the playboy mentality could not get, or did not wait and work long enough to get, through the legislative process close to the majority of the people, it got through the Courts, the most vulnerable area in the system.

Privatism Breaks Through

In order to interpret puritan individualism in the light of playboy selfism, the Court needed an appropriate innovation. Individual liberty always existed in tension with social responsibility. But liberty was never before involved in an ethic of pleasure and play. Sexual pleasure separated from commitment—in other words, sexual privatism—was a playboy innovation. *Privatism, a gross exaggeration of authentic privacy*, became the interpreting device applied by the Court to the Constitution.

How did the Court *discover* playboy privatism in a Constitution that was formed without any playboy intentions?

As the rhetoric of the "wanted and unwanted child" became increasingly more shrill in the playboy culture, the force of this rhetoric began to be felt in the Court. Finally, as the sexual revolution neared its peak, the playboy mentality, through an individual case, made its first, careful, constitutional move.

In the 1965 *Griswold v. Connecticut* decision, a Connecticut law making it a criminal misdemeanor to "use any drug, medicinal article or instrument for the purpose of preventing conception" was struck down. This was the first "privacy" case based on what the Court called a "zone of privacy," meaning the marital bedroom in the private realm of the family.

The newly formed concept of privacy, though not mentioned in the Constitution, appeared to be rooted in the Fourth Amendment's protection against unreasonable searches and seizures. This protection seemed to the Court to include conjugal rights.

On the face of the decision, the Court did not appear to enshrine the right to contraception in the Constitution directly. The Justices were supposedly protecting the family zone of life, as the Constitution is meant to do.

But the subsequent judicial impulse clearly opposed the traditional family, and favored radical selfism instead. Only seven years after the first privacy decision sanctioned marital contraception, the 1972 *Eisenstadt v. Baird* decision struck down a Massachusetts law that prohibited the distribution of contraceptives to the unmarried.

The family "zone of privacy" was expanded into an individual "right of privacy." Rights previously found within the privacy of marriage were gratuitously extended to the unmarried.

The selfism of the playboy culture broke through *Griswold's* vulnerable "zone of privacy" and became, in *Eisenstadt*, outright privatism.

The newly formulated "right to privacy" of the individual was an invention to accommodate the genital activity of the unmarried. The playboy and playmate had gained what was construed to be a constitutional right to separate sex from the family, a separation the puritan would have found unthinkable.

In the case for unmarried sex, Justice William Brennan said, "If the right to privacy means anything, it is the right of the *individual,* married or single, to be free from unwarranted governmental intrusion into matters so fundamentally affecting a person as the decision whether to bear or beget a child." The word "individual" was italicized by Brennan to emphasize that having children is no longer to be regarded as a family matter.

This judgment was a raw judicial intrusion into the privacy of the family, ironically done in the name of privacy. But the *meaning* of privacy had changed so much from one point to the other that it seemed to become two words instead of one. The first meaning referred to the family; the other referred only to the individual.

Since the particular individual who ties sex to pregnancy is the female, the next Court decision, the 1973 *Roe v. Wade* abortion decision, was based on the individual privacy of the female.

The outcome of the abortion decision was already implied in the rationale for the previous (1972) defense of contraceptives for the unmarried. In fact, according to John Noonan in his book, *A Private Choice,* the contraception case was decided only after the abortion case had been argued before the Court. He says that the revolutionary rationale in the contraception decision was probably invented as a needed precedent for the subsequent abortion decision.[3]

In any event, the 1972 decision favoring contraception for singles was the only true precedent for the abortion decision (Noonan).

Both decisions were based on a society of isolated selfists. Instead of regarding the family as a natural bonding of individuals in a basic social unit to be protected by the State, the Court now implied that the State no longer presupposes, nor protects, the family.

Starting, in 1965, with the intent to protect the privacy of marriage, the Court radicalized privacy so far as to legalize free-choice abortion throughout the full term of pregnancy, and to pit wife against husband and daughter against parents.

Four days before the 1976 Bicentennial celebration, in *Planned Parenthood v. Danforth,* the Court denied the father any rights in a woman's abortion decision, and denied the parents of a minor daughter any significant rights in her abortion decision. Finally, *Colautti v. Franklin* (1979) declared that legally prescribed attempts to save the baby's life in an abortion interfered with the abortionist's right to practice.

This whole train of rulings solidly installed the playboy mentality in the official interpretation of the Constitution.

Between the 1965 contraception case and the 1973 abortion case, a volcanic kind of logic moved relentlessly toward its conclusion. By 1973, the full force of the playboy culture exploded in what dissenting Justice Byron White called "an improvident and extravagant exercise of the power of judicial review." He also said, "I find nothing in the language or history of the Constitution to suggest the Court's judgment. The Court simply fashions and announces a new constitutional right."[4]

The device which the Justices used to pry their train of playboy decisions from the Constitution—their novel notion of privacy—nowhere mentioned in the Constitution's written words, was not even suggested. The puritan concept of privacy, a concept authentically implied in the founding document, included the right to private property, and to privacy of family and religion. Sexual privacy was strictly established on its family basis.

Self-serving privatism, a playboy intrusion into the family, had to be "amended" into the Constitution. The result raised the individual to absolute supremacy over the family, effectively destroying natural, pre-Constitutional family bonds. The privacy of puritan individualism became the privacy of playboy selfism.

Influenced by the overwhelming impulsiveness of the playboy culture, and the power of its scripts blaring in the media, the Court, too, became impulsive. Acting more on impulse (predilection) than on judicial wisdom, this eminent branch of government moved to satisfy the playmate's shrill demands for the liberty to "control my own body." Doing so, the Court lost its ability to control its own judicial body. It slipped into an impulsive interpretation of liberty, and read that hapless view into the Constitution's provision for individual freedom.

The Court's metamorphosis of liberty was accomplished by shifting what is traditionally within the scope of public morality (the right to life) into the scope of individual privacy. This spurious move had the effect of deeply weakening limits on the individual's privacy. What else could now be moved from public jurisdiction to private freedom of choice?

The same Court that arbitrarily invented constitutional privatism must also arbitrarily limit that "privacy" or else accept its absolute implications. Privatism has no inherent limits of its own. Since the Court has not provided these limits, the Constitution now carries the immense burden of a free-floating, rootless right to privacy, a right that tends to grow like a cancer.

Such a counterfeit right was given by seven of nine men, not directly to men, but to women. This so-called right would not have been given to women, however, unless it directly served male interests of the playboy kind.

A Woman's Right to Choose

The new "right of privacy" was based on pregnancy management for selfists, not on the dignity of women as persons, nor on the dignity of the family as the basic unit of society. The all-male Court was caught in the mounting pressure of the playboy culture as it broke away from the sexual moralism of the previous culture. The playmate's cries for the legal right to control her own body, sounding like music to playboy ears, found men ready and willing to rally to her cause. The "privacy" decisions boldly served playboy interests by awarding Constitutional protection to the playboy's desire for sex freed from all family responsibilities. These decisions facilitated the playboy culture's formation of the playmate, without whom there could be no fully functioning playboy.

Because sex is bound to pregnancy in the female, the playboy-conditioned Court was compelled to center the separation of sex from the family in the woman's freedom of choice, and further compelled, in subsequent decisions, to separate the woman from her husband, and the dependent daughter from her parents. Isolated from the family, the female now became dependent on the medical profession as a family substitute. The privacy of the woman and her mate in the bedroom was eclipsed by her privacy with her doctor (usually a total stranger who often does not even see her face) in a public abortion facility. The "disease" caused in her body by her male partner could now be legally "corrected" by a professional controller of disease who is willing to serve playboy interests.

This radical separation of the woman from her family is not something that could be found in a Constitution founded and supported by a puritan culture. The puritan woman was contained within the family: the legally protected private domain of the male. So the new supremacy of the medical profession over the family in a woman's generative role had to be a Court contrivance. In this judicial scheme, the female's partnership with her husband was transferred to a new partnership with her doctor instead.

As the Court's bonding of the woman with a disease-controlling institution did not enhance her dignity as a woman, neither did her newly established puritan elitism. The woman was allowed to take her place among the elect. She was permitted to become a free-choice destroyer of the "fetuses" as the previous elect had been free-choice slayers of the "savages" and owners and destroyers of the "niggers." She was now enshrined in the highest law of the land as a perfect likeness of the wanting and unwanting God at the foundation of our culture.

Based on the new "fetal tissue" theory of pregnancy, a theory peculiar to the playboy mentality, the disease-correcting institution of medicine was allowed to treat the result of a female's copulation with her partner as if it were a growing malignancy whenever it was unwanted. Something radical happened to degrade a woman's normal, natural, and healthy fertility, and thus to degrade the woman herself.

Historically, in tribal cultures, human fertility was so important and mysterious that it was surrounded with magic, religious rituals, and even human sacrifice. In post-tribal civilized cultures, fertility no longer was a magic or religious matter, but still was valued as somehow related to the sacred.

In the playboy culture, fertility is dissociated from the sacred, and is associated, instead, with disease or malignancy. Fertility is not regarded as a gift of the gods, nor as a gift of God

100

through created nature, but as a *medical problem* to be solved. Human perception of the sacredness of fertility has now given way to the sacredness of contraception, sterilization, and abortion.

None of the above perceptions of fertility (whether associated with magic and ritual, or with "don't touch" and "don't talk about" Victorian sacredness, or with prescriptions and surgery) treat it as an integral power of sexual adults.

Balanced minds see human fertility as a natural and healthy power of the whole person. Unbalanced, impulsive, playboy-playmate minds, on the other hand, demand a constitutionally protected prescriber or surgeon to "control" a woman's generative potential for her. She is not recognized as one who is *able* to regulate her fertility by herself.

By lock-stepping the woman with her physician, the Court was not acknowledging her dignity as a person, but was adjusting to something construed as defective in her nature: her inconvenient tendency to produce unwanted "fetal tissue" as a result of her sexual contact with an "infecting" male.

Nor was such a use of medical procedures designed to recognize the physician's dignity as a healer. Doctors who treat normal, healthy physical conditions as if they were deformed are practicing quackery.

There are good, noble physicians who recognize better ways of responding to an untimely pregnancy. These ways might not be easy or lucrative. But, as everyone knows, quacks deal in the easy and the lucrative instead of the wise and the true.

Nor was such an adjustment to "depravity" in a woman's nature inspired by a sense of the dignity of the male as a person. The playboy culture's rape of the human generative power in both women and men was motivated by *a profound hopelessness about the human person's ability to regulate sexual expression; it was inspired by a deep sense of sexual helplessness.*

A Man's Inability to Choose

The Court's abortion decisions rendered all males under its jurisdiction legally impotent in their generative role. Even the legal husband was constitutionally relegated to a "child"-male or playboy status, the condition of one who has no direct interest in a playmate's pregnancy potential.

That millions of married men have taken this attack on their generative power with so much lethargic acquiescence shows the mind-binding effect of cultural scripts, and the overwhelming pervasiveness of the playboy mentality. Many of these men would vote against abortion. But their spirit is so decimated by the culture that they have little energy to protest, other than that needed to pull a lever in a voting booth.

Only the woman is legally allowed to choose. Her male partner, even if he is the father of a family, has no legal power in her wanting and unwanting role.

This is the price the playboy is all too willing to pay for his ideological control over women's bodies both in the bedroom and in the public "cleanup" facility. This is the way he wants it to be! And he will continue to fight in court to keep it that way.

The Unwanted Child

When the "right to privacy" was expanded to include what is called termination of pregnancy, the woman was given permission to make this decision for any reason of convenience through six months of pregnancy. The states were given permission to protect the viable child during the last three months of pregnancy, but *were not required* to do so. This meant that, according to the Constitution, the viable child *need not be protected at all*. If this child's life could be terminated successfully, any time before birth, such an action could be legally warranted.

The states were virtually free to allow abortions until birth. Their "freedom" to protect life in the last three months of pregnancy was only apparent. The Court allowed states to legislate against abortion in the last trimester of gestation, except for cases involving maternal health. But in *Roe v. Wade's* companion case, *Doe v. Bolton,* health was defined so broadly as to include "all factors—physical, emotional, psychological, and the woman's age—relevant to her well-being." The word "health" practically meant "convenience."

No national television or newspaper network reported the full extent of the abortion decisions. Repeatedly, for years, the media generally reported only abortion on demand for the first three months of pregnancy. Why only part of the truth? Was the Court's legislation so radical and sweeping that the media of the playboy culture, in order to safeguard the playboy "victory," felt instinctively constrained to suppress its full impact?

Due to their overwhelming interest in privatism, the 7-2 majority of the Court showed no real interest in the prenatal child. This was the case on numerous counts.

First, *Roe v. Wade* said *the Constitution does not mention the unborn as persons.* Then it appealed to the right of privacy. But *the Constitution does not mention privacy either.*

Second, *Roe v. Wade* quotes an abortion advocate, Lawrence Lader, repeatedly, but does not quote, even once, a world-renowned fetologist such as Albert Liley.

Third, in a desperate groping for precedents, the Court's opinion writer apparently assumed that the most ancient is the most absolute, and referred to ancient pagan religions which did not bar abortions. The subsequent life-protecting views of Hippocrates, Pythagoras, and Christianity, though more advanced, were brushed aside as mere cultural manifestos, not expressions of an absolute medical ethics. The Court's writer did not stop to reflect long enough to see what a massive cultural manifesto the *Roe v. Wade* opinion was to represent.

Fourth, in spite of scientific knowledge that the prenatal child sucks his or her thumb by ten to twelve weeks after conception, the Justices said they did not know whether the life of this being had begun. They called it "potential life," and therefore "not a person in the whole sense."

Fifth, by saying they did not know when human life begins, the Justices contradicted themselves when they went ahead and ruled as if they knew for certain that life does not begin before birth.

Such a bizarre exercise of the human mind, as these points show, could not pass unnoticed, even by lawyers who agreed with the abortion liberty. Soon after the decision was handed down, John Hart Ely, in an article in the *Yale Law Journal*, criticized the reasoning used, while saying that he supported abortion.[5]

The playboy-influenced Justices were so interested in the newly devised concept of privacy that they conceded intellectual impotence before the question of life's beginning. It was a strategic helplessness: without it the overwhelming power they gave to privatism would not have been possible.

The same kind of mentality, in its puritan phase, that could see nothing in natural humanity but a "savage beast," could see nothing more in prenatal existence than fetal tissue or "potential life." The "beast" that could be saved only by being wanted in spite of this degraded condition became the "fetus" that could live only by being wanted in spite of being nothing more than just a "fetus."

In both the slavery and abortion decisions, the slave and fetus were regarded as non-persons, the better to treat them as property.

The supremacy of property over personhood appears in the legal right of the unborn child to inherit property. The child has property rights but has no right to life or to personhood.

Wanting and unwanting is legitimate in the realm of property; it is intolerable in the realm of personhood. Persons, if they are to be treated acceptably as wanted or unwanted material, must be reduced to the level of property.

The Real Constitution and the Child

A balanced mind might possibly say that it does not know when life begins. But this mind would be keenly aware of the significant event that takes place when a human ovum receives a human sperm. This event initiates individual development as an unbroken trajectory continuing through birth all the way to death in old age (when this continuum is not interrupted by premature death).

No person is a grownup ovum or a grownup sperm. Each person is, quite obviously, a grownup entity that results when the sperm penetrates the ovum. A balanced, healthy mind would realize that an individual's life begins in his or her own single-celled beginning.

When asked whether this incipient life is human, a balanced, rational mind notes that no plant or animal cell ever has been found within this life. Furthermore, when confronted with the usual "body-soul" talk, the rational mind realizes that the body cannot exist, much less develop as a human body, without a human soul, not even in its progression from one to two cells.

The soul is present in prenatal development just as it is when we are asleep or comatose. Body and soul are vitally integral, not mechanically added one to the other.

Is the single-celled individual right after conception a human person? No rational mind can say with certainty that the individual at conception is *not* a person. Such an unwarranted conclusion would be similar to that of a judge saying in court, "I don't know whether you are innocent, therefore you are guilty." "I don't know when human life begins, therefore it does not begin before birth (or viability or _____)."

Under the Constitution, a person is assumed to be innocent until proven guilty—beyond a reasonable doubt. In harmony with this humane and rational standard of government, it would seem reasonable that a person should be assumed to exist from the single-celled beginning of individual development until proven otherwise beyond a reasonable doubt.

Has anyone ever proven beyond a reasonable doubt that a person *does not exist* at conception? Some have tried to prove that a person does not exist at conception by defining implantation as conception, and by using twinning as evidence for their assumptions.[6] But no one has succeeded in finding such a proof.

The concept of a "potential person" implies that personhood depends on development rather than on being. Actually there is no such thing as a potential person, only a tiny person with great potential.

If there is a reasonable doubt about a person's existence, the balanced, rational mind always grants the benefit of the doubt. When a mine caves in, people do not stand around outside the mine and say the trapped miners are dead. They assume the miners are alive until proven dead or unreachable. And they act accordingly.

Furthermore, a sane approach to the abortion question would notice how the Declaration of Independence states that all humans are created equal, not born equal. A balanced mind notices the clear implication that equality begins with creation, not with birth.

Because the Constitution does not define the prenatal child as a citizen (only those "born or naturalized in the United States" are citizens), the interpreters assumed that the prenatal child is not a person according to the Constitution. This confusion of personhood with citizenship is elitist at best.

Obviously, one can be a natural person without being a citizen. A natural person therefore can exist before as well as after birth. Obviously, too, the Constitution does not identify natural personhood with citizenship. Otherwise alien residents and foreign visitors could not be constitutionally recognized as natural persons.

The Justices had no reason to assume that, according to the Constitution, personhood begins at birth.

A balanced, rational mind would have regarded natural personhood as something *presupposed* by the Constitution. However, both the slavery and the abortion decisions identified natural personhood with citizenship, and used this irrationality to relegate the degraded natural person to the status of property.

The real Constitution supports the benefit of the doubt on the question of natural personhood. But the Court, in its abortion decisions, assumed that natural personhood is conferred by the State, and that it is given, rather than presupposed, by the Constitution.

Since natural personhood in prenatal individuals is not mentioned, the Court then assumed that these individuals are not protected by the Constitution. The idea seems to be that natural personhood exists only where there is a compelling state interest. This is nothing short of judicial tyranny.

In the 1976 Danforth decision, the Court said the father has no right to interfere in the woman's abortion decision because the State cannot grant the father this right. It is true that the father's natural right to his generative role does not come from the State. But the Court *used* this fact to take away the father's natural rights instead of protecting these rights as it should.

The abortion decisions therefore invented a totalitarian concept of both the State and the Constitution. The implication for other lives besides those in the womb is as broad as the Court's distended notion of individual privacy and the peculiar notion of choice that is involved in this privacy.

The Unwanted Parent

If the culture of the unwanted child is allowed to run its course, it is destined to become a culture of the unwanted parent. The same concepts that permit unwanting parents to destroy their children can become, *at will*, concepts permitting unwanting children to destroy their parents.

"After all," selfist minds might ask, "why limit viability to a biological definition? Isn't there also psychological and social viability? Don't psychological and social support-systems function like wombs? When lives become meaningless and socially nonviable, why not painless removal? Why not legalize euthanasia for the elderly, senile, and handicapped? A constitutional precedent already exists."

By violating, in *Roe v. Wade,* the Constitution's *presupposed* meaning of natural personhood, the Supreme Court not only allowed abortion until birth, but also identified the meaning of natural personhood with the ability to live a "meaningful life."

The Justices were not interested in human life as such. They were interested only in "viable" human beings that have, as they called it, the "capability of meaningful life." Only these must be protected by the State.

And the Court purposely connected "meaningful life" with privatism, convenience, and choice—an ominous implication for anyone not considered, by choice, convenient or viable.

Statistics show that by the year 2005 there will be 50 million people over 65 years of age. The tax base for supporting their needs will be no larger than it is today. As the young are being destroyed, and as the population ages, pressures to legalize euthanasia and suicide are bound to increase.

Children naturally learn from their parents. And so the unwanting child who learned his or her way of thinking from unwanting parents is well-prepared for the next stage ahead of us. Without a breakthrough into a new mentality, the "wanting and unwanting" breakdown in our unbalanced masculine culture is likely to continue.

Summary

As these chapters on puritanism have shown, a mentality strongly tends to work itself out in the events of history. If the mentality lacks the feminine principle of integration, its results in history only make explicit this lack of integration.

The absence of feminine receptivity in the puritan mind, and consequently in the puritan God, eventually made the feminine person, the woman, an image and likeness of that too masculine mind and too masculine God. The absent feminine side eventually became the dominant female in the wanting and unwanting role that gave the male no power in the choice. The masculine dominance of the hard, cold divinity who had absolute power to choose whomever he would, eventually became the absent male who had no legal power in the wanting and unwanting choice.

In other words, one extreme converted itself into the opposite extreme. Feminine absence became dominance in women. And masculine dominance became absence in men.

Such an oscillating inversion of extremes is inevitable in a civilization that does not admit receptivity into its mentality. This civilization lacks the very thing that unites opposites and changes them from extremes in a conflict to elements that work together in harmony and peace.

PART THREE

FINDING A NEW BEGINNING

CHAPTER NINE

TIME FOR A BETTER WAY

We have seen how the absence of the feminine side of the mind in puritanism generated a masculine reaction that affected more than four centuries of Western history. From the cold, arbitrary choices of the puritan God to the impulsive "right to choose" now lodged in the American Constitution, we have been, and still are, caught in the driven forces of that masculine reaction. Liberation from its drive is the *real* question of women's liberation. And also of men's.

As Genesis says, "It is not good for man to be alone." Neither is it good for the masculine side of the mind to be alone in the processes that form a civilization. When that happens, scientific technology charges ahead without wisdom, and becomes steadily more dehumanizing and dangerous. The survival of the entire planet becomes an awesome everyday question.

Let's see, as clearly as possible, what caused the problem, the better to find a true solution. The cause exists in a faulty relationship between the feminine and masculine sides of the mind.

The feminine side, in both women and men, has a receptive sense of *being*. The masculine side has an expressive sense of *doing*. The first says, "You are good just because you are." The second says, "You are good if you *do* good and avoid evil." Both approaches are needed, and equally so.

But if we hear only the second, more obvious, voice, and not the first, we tend to think that our goodness depends entirely on our actions. We become too action-oriented.

The Healing Power of Affirmation

We need to hear the first voice first: "You are good just because you are you." When we really hear this voice well, and feel secure in its emphasis, then we are able to hear the second voice well: "You are good because you do what is good." Then we can become more balanced, integrated, and whole.

The feminine voice that responds to the goodness of being is an affirming voice.[1] The masculine voice that attends to the character of our actions is a firming voice.

Firming is meant to be included within af-firming, just as our actions are meant to come from within us.

Affirmation that clearly includes what we might call firmation is both feminine and masculine at once. It is integrated in a beautiful and powerful way. Affirmation is the *root* answer to the problem of disintegration that besets our individual lives as well as our culture and civilization.

The feminine side of affirmation is active, not passive. It is a *receptive* response to the goodness of being; an inner readiness of the heart, not an outward performance. Nevertheless, this spontaneous response of the heart warms our outward actions, while, at the same time, it moves into the masculine side of affirmation and becomes firm with our actions.

Someone who is affirming, but who is also permissive and says, "Do what you feel like doing," is not really affirming at all. This person lacks a sense of good actions versus bad actions (not all actions are good). The permissive attitude fails to see our need for good actions, and how these express and enhance the goodness of our being. Bad actions have a frustrating, disintegrating effect.

Unconditional love for the being of a person is a feminine quality in men as well as women. Conditional approval for that person's actions is a masculine quality. Both qualities are necessary for affirmation, and equally so.

Affirmation, then, is a healing paradox. It is both unconditional and conditional at once. When this crucial union of opposites breaks down, we find ourselves sinking into the tortures of conflicting extremes. And there we stay until we recover the original paradox again.

When, at the time of the Renaissance, the feminine voice became steadily weaker, the masculine voice that says, "*Do* this; don't *do* that," became just as steadily louder. When the "do's and don'ts" reached a frenzy, people rightly sensed the futility of trying to make themselves good in the "goodness vacuum" left by the absent feminine voice. Instead of *listening* for that voice and *letting* the vacuum be filled (listening and letting are receptive), people heard a hardening in the masculine voice.

In the form of Calvinism, this masculine voice said, "You are no good at all. There is nothing you can do to make yourself good. You can only be wanted or unwanted, in spite of your wretchedness. You cannot even know whether you are wanted unless your actions are morally correct. But these actions cannot enhance a goodness you do not really have, even if you are wanted. You must force (sheer willpower) your evil nature to do good actions. But these actions can do nothing more than *prove* that you are wanted in spite of your unlovableness."

In this sad situation, the relation of doing to being was totally out of joint. The relation of the masculine to the feminine was broken. And so it has remained.

Finding a better way means listening, once again, to the lost feminine voice. Deep, quiet, intent listening. New life means letting the feminine voice fill the emptiness that waits. "You are good because you exist. Receive in joy the gift of your being."

When the feminine voice returns and is fully heard, we can then hear the masculine voice within the context of the feminine. Then our actions do not have to prove anything. They simply

115

express, enhance, and develop our being. And they do this under the guidance of truth and firmness in our values.

Being is the source of *power* for action. *Receiving our being* as it is given gives us power. The power that comes from receptivity makes the difference between potency and impotence in whatever we do.

"Do this; don't do that," is heard in the context of "You are good because you are you." This relation of action to being is the source of true human potency, sexually as well as spiritually. *Being* love is the source of power for *making* love. True performance comes from the receptivity of love, and not from the will to prove oneself.

Male potency on the level of the mind and civilization, as well as in physical sexuality, requires a healthy union of the masculine with the feminine. The absence of the feminine side of the mind undoes the masculine side. Unless power and performance come from the capacity to receive power from being, these masculine qualities cannot function well.

A civilization of outgoing power and performance without ingoing receptivity—like puritan civilization —misses the feminine side of everything in life, including the warmth and intimacy of God. Subsequently, we experience the chilling effect of a too-masculine God on our sense of the universe and ourselves within it.

Beyond the Puritan God

One of the first blessings of a mentality that regains the feminine side of the mind is a rediscovery of the affirming God of persons, and the passing away of the severe, remote God of puritanism. The announcement, in the late 1960s by some theologians, that "God is dead," is good news if the dead God is the Lord of arbitrary, willful choice that took hold of the conscious and unconscious mind of a nation and the interpretation of its Constitution.

It might seem questionable to trace the wanting and unwanting philosophy of our own day back to the puritan sense of an arbitrary and willful God. But anyone who realizes the formative influence of a religious ideology within a culture, knows that the puritan God is not dead in America today, at least not in the subconscious mind of our culture. Even American atheists, though they might deny it, are "children" of this God.

The religious viewpoint and sentiment of a culture affects the very roots of that culture's psychological, sociological, and economic character. As Max Weber has shown, the religion of the elect affected even the character of American capitalism.

This observation is not meant to imply that capitalism must be abolished along with the puritan sense of God, anymore than it means that the Constitution must be abolished. As previously shown, good things came from puritan initiatives. The challenge, now, is to reassess our sense of God as well as our cultural character, and to incorporate the good qualities of our culture into another, more integrative spirit.

Most Western religions (Jewish, Catholic, and Protestant) have the God of persons in their original faith. This personal God, vividly present, for example, in the evangelical faith, appears in *Genesis* responding to all things in an affirming way, and repeating like a chant, "It is good." "It is good."

The puritans could not hear this voice very well. Feeling deeply depraved, rather than deprived, by sin, they lost the affirming God of *Genesis*. As a result of this spiritual chilling, the universe changed from being a home for persons, to becoming, for the people of the Enlightenment, a cold, mechanistic, mathematical machine. The dominion given to us by God changed from a caring stewardship to a self-proving domination.

In contrast to those influenced by the God of performance and domination, Mother Teresa of Calcutta, sensitive to the more feminine side of life, has been quoted as saying, "We are not called to be successful, but to be faithful."

The one true God is radically personal, but also lawgiving. The affirming God of persons says an unconditional yes to the

117

goodness of creatures, and, at the same time, a firm no to some of the things some of these creatures can do. The Ten Commandments issue this definite no.

The unconditional lover of persons is, at the same time, a conditional lover of their actions. We cannot affirm someone if we think anything they choose to do, just because they choose it, is fine with us. Crucially and most significantly, affirmation is opposed to arbitrary choice.

Because people are basically good, even in the state of original sin, what they *do* once they are baptized allows them to participate in their salvation. This is why evil actions are forbidden by God. These freely chosen actions lead us away from salvation, not because God ceases to love unconditionally, but because the sinner refuses to receive this love. Such a refusal is forbidden. However, the love that forbids also forgives. The one who refuses can repent.

Human nature is crippled by original sin, but it is not totally depraved as the puritans thought. The tendency we have to refuse to receive the gift of finite being, and to want to become like God in the wrong way, is an original distortion in us that alienates us from God. This alienation weakens our natural powers, but does not destroy them.

Anyone who has a self-proving sense of self, and wants to be the source of his or her own goodness, cannot relate well with the affirming God. The reason is that the self-prover lacks a truly receptive attitude toward God's affirming presence.

Just as we receive our being from our Creator, we need to receive our salvation. But what kind of receiving? Passive or active?

If we are totally ruined by original sin, we are totally passive in relation to God. But if our being is still good, though deeply weakened and distorted, we are still able to be active in relation to God, with God's help. Only an active kind of receiving makes cooperation possible. Without it we are spiritually impotent.

We cannot be saved by our own power. Once salvation is offered to us, however, we cannot be saved without our willing cooperation. We are not spiritually impotent.

The God of persons is also the God of actions. But the feminine emphasis on the being of the person precedes, and includes, the masculine emphasis on the person's actions. Even in God, actions come from being.

When the feminine and masculine become integrated within us, in the image and likeness of the affirming God, everything in our lives, including our national character, can be favorably affected.

The Warming of America

The masculine reaction that begot puritanism produced a powerful form of individualism that identified us more with what we do than with who we are. Individualism is not based on the primacy of the person. A performance-centered culture is not a person-centered culture.

The word individual means one among many. A pebble on the ground is one among many. So the person, while being an individual, is much more than just an individual.

A person is one who is capable of loving many. To be a person is to be alone and together at once: a paradox. A person is autonomous and, at the same time, intimately related.

A society of individualists tends to become a kind of collective, rather than a community of persons. Democracy and communism are different kinds of collective. In a democratic collective, the state serves the individual; government is of, by, and for the individual. In a communist collective, the individual serves the state. Both kinds of collective, without the primacy of the person, are masculine opposites. While the democratic collective is able to shift into the modality of personhood, the communistic collective is incapable of such a shift as long as the individual is made to serve the state.

A collective is based on individuals; a community is based on persons. The collective is artificial and humanly made like a suit of clothes. The community is natural, and is more like a living thing than an artifact. A community is a group of persons (relational autonomies) who share purposes and values in concrete ways.

The warming of America means a growing sense of community between persons, and a gradual lessening of our tough individualism. This growing sense of community does not imply a growing welfare state, but rather an increase in mutually volunteered help and support.

Everything a *person* feels, thinks, and does affects, in some way, the community. And vice versa. Person and community relate in a kind of organic way.

In the American collective, most of what an *individual* feels, thinks, and does is his or her own business, and is seen as private, separate from the community, and supposedly affecting no one else. Choice based on individualism is not the same as choice based on a true sense of the person.

Individualism separates private and public morality, and puts them in closed-off compartments. Person-centered morality sees the private and the public as united in their difference, rather than as separate.

While person-centered morality includes authentic privacy, it does not recognize such a thing as a separate private morality. *No morality is private, even when it is personal.* Authentic privacy is always integral with social morality. A healthy society depends on a healthy sense of personal integrity even in that person's most hidden privacy.

As we have seen earlier, individualism is not a secure support for the family. Only a person-centered awareness is able to integrate the feminine and masculine sides of human nature, and, as a result, able to integrate the child and parent aspects. Unity within each person, and between persons, is the key to the family. The *affirming person,* not the *performing individual*, is the uniting power.

Performance and individualism have their place and their value. A person-centered life supports a moderated form of individualism, and encourages excellence in the kind of performance and achievement that enhances, not detracts from, the good of persons and families.

As a new sense of the person emerges in our national awareness, interpretations of the Constitution can become more sensitive to persons and families. Our Constitution needs person and family amendments to balance its emphasis, and to warm its individualism.

Greater attunement to the feminine does not mean that our Constitution needs the Equal Rights Amendment, as this amendment is now formed with its masculine way of thinking about equality. The masculine logic of identity versus separation is inclined to reduce women into sameness with men. Reducing women and men to "people" in a sexless way is not the answer. Same pay for same work (if dependability is commensurate) is a matter of justice, but is not the main issue of an equality amendment. Another formulation, based on a more sensitive and paradoxical way of thinking, would be better. But this needed way of thinking is not yet developed in our culture.

Alvin Toffler's idea in *The Third Wave* that we should start over from the beginning and construct a new Constitution seems too radically masculine. "If we begin now," Toffler says, "we and our children can take part in the exciting reconstruction not merely of our obsolete political structures, but of civilization itself."[2]

Taking apart a structure and building another is appropriate if the structure is a building that needs to be replaced. But social structures are not brick and mortar buildings, nor are they merely logical arrangements. They are people-structures even when they are social inventions. They require an integrated approach to organization and change.

What we need, instead of a new Constitution, is a God-person-and-family-centered culture that would amend favorably, and influence positively the *interpretation* of, the Constitution we already have.

We do not have to reconstitute civilization. We need renewal and reorientation instead.

We need a new mentality "in the air we breathe." The needed way of thinking and living is one that begins in the feminine side of the mind, and stays securely in the feminine while it expands into the masculine. This new mentality then brings the masculine and feminine into union with, not identification with, each other.

As reorientation takes place, some old structures can be dismantled, and some new ones can be created. But awareness about the person and the family already present in our culture in a rudimentary way, and the need of this awareness for wise nurturing, can moderate the raw male impetus to take over the scene, or to tear down and rebuild.

The puritan archetype will always be with us. But if we become aware of this image and its deeply pervasive mentality in our national character, if we maintain this awareness at all times, and if we clearly see the puritan shadow as well as its light, we can see new radiance, and feel new warmth in our land. As the sun shines more fully, the shadow recedes.

CHAPTER TEN

HOW TO LIVE WITH OUR FEELINGS

Beyond the puritan and playboy shadows in our lives, we can find a better way of living with our feelings. We can learn to let our feelings and emotions be what they are without imposing our values on them (like the puritan) or deriving our values from them (like the playboy).

Letting our feelings be, and be what they are, begins in the receptive side of the mind. *We learn to let our own self be, then we can let our feelings be.* We receive the gift of existence into awareness, and we let ourselves experience how good it is just to exist.

Usually this moment of clear, calm reality happens when we are doing nothing but be-ing. Actively, not passively. As the ancient saying goes, "The way to do is to be."

Without the healing experience of be-ing, we have a hard time letting out feelings just be, and be what they are. As a result, we feel impelled or compelled toward outward action. Our freedom to act or not to act is diminished.

If we are afraid of letting go and receiving the gift of being from the Giver, we are afraid of the feminine. We are stalled. We are Eve after she lost everything, and could not regain anything. We are Adam alienated from the feminine. We are cast out of the garden of being. And we are failing to receive the second gift: our redemption.

Begin here, in the capacity for receiving the gift. Or there can be no beginning at all.

Here in this deep inner beginning, we receive the affirming love of God. The Eve in us needs to receive. There is nowhere else to go. There is no better way.

When we let go and receive the gift of being, and the affirming love that gives this gift, we feel no need to prove to ourselves, nor to anyone else, that we are good. Even if we are sick or crippled and cannot do much of anything, we are good because we are.

When we let ourselves experience our goodness, we can then have our feelings without impulsion or compulsion. We can receive the spontaneous part of our self—our feelings and emotions—as valuable energy for deepening our inner life, not just for outward expression. This healthy relation to our spontaneity requires awareness of what is going on within.

There is a part of our self that becomes *aware*. There is another part that *feels,* and still another part that *cares.* These three aspects of our inner life are so basic that we can call them *selves* to emphasize their importance. But each of us is just one self, with three special resources for learning how to live well with our feelings.

Our Spontaneous Self

"When I jump into the water, I feel cold." "Looking into the refrigerator makes me feel hungry." "Hot, humid weather is depressing." "Whenever you say that about my friend, it makes me angry." "A short prayer often calms my fears."

Our lives are full of happy and sad, comfortable and uncomfortable, satisfied and unsatisfied feelings. These are spontaneous responses to whatever touches or moves us in any way. Feelings let us know our state of being. They tell us what we need, and they warn us of danger. Uncomfortable feelings like anger are just as important as comfortable ones like contentment. Anger gives us energy to do something about the evils in life. Fear warns us of danger, and gives us energy to escape. Joy tells us that life is good, and gives us energy to live a fuller life.

We can easily acknowledge that happy, comfortable, and satisfied feelings are good. It seems quite easy to let them be, and be what they are. But sadness, pain, rage, fear, and panic can seem intolerable. How can we just let them be?

In his book called *Feeling Good About Feeling Bad,* Dr. Paul Warner, a psychiatrist, says, "Even the very uncomfortable feelings such as pain, severe grief, and panic can be modified to a more tolerable level by planning on them and accepting them."[1] These feelings, too, are good—in a paradoxical way. Suffering can deepen our perceptions and make us more receptive.

It is good to feel pain when something is wrong so we can take action to correct its cause. The pain itself seems bad, however, and relief from it seems good. Sometimes pain is chronic, and might not be relieved by anything. Learning to let it be is a special challenge.

Spontaneous responses to life—our feelings—are physical, emotional, mental, and spiritual. Hunger and thirst, for example, are physical. Delight and fear are emotional. Peace of mind is a mental feeling. Love of God is spiritual.

Emotions are a psychological, not physical, kind of feeling. Emotions have a physical component, however, and directly affect our physical life. Physical feelings like hunger, thirst, and tiredness can stimulate emotional feelings like sadness and frustration. And we can eat, drink, and sleep for emotional, not just physical, reasons.

Feelings and Actions

Some of our feelings tell us what we *must* do to stay alive. Physical feelings of hunger, thirst, and tiredness need to be satisfied necessarily. But we can eat, drink, and sleep too much, too little, or just enough. We can make choices about our biological need-feelings.

While some of our feelings necessarily urge us to act, others, such as sexual and angry feelings, do not, even though they have strong physical components. We can feel anger just as much as sexual desire in our bodies. Sometimes people get red in the face and physically tense when they are angry. They might even feel like going into physical action, striking or knocking down the object of their anger. But they do not do so just because they feel like it.

There are times when sexual and angry feelings appropriately lead to physical expression. What about the times when such expression is not appropriate? What should we do, for example, when we feel like bursting into physical violence against another person?

These feelings generate impulses to act. While letting ourselves feel intensely angry, we can hold back our impulses and use their energy to make our mind start working creatively. We can think about a better way to express our anger. This powerful emotion is a valuable source of energy for figuring out the best way to express what we feel, for growing within as a person, and for relating well with other people.

At first, outward action (defensive or offensive) seems like the main reason why we have feelings of anger. But the ability of these feelings to increase awareness, sensitivity, thoughtfulness, and responsibility is their main purpose, not outward expression.

Anger has an outward purpose, but only when it is appropriate. Anger can inspire us to do everything in our power to right a wrong in a constructive way. We can express anger in assertive words if not in actions. But we do not have to use even words in order to grow within and to remain emotionally healthy.

Dr. Conrad W. Baars, a psychiatrist, tells of his experience with a powerful feeling of anger which he felt, but could not express in any way, for two years. He was caught and imprisoned by the Nazis during World War II when he was helping downed Allied flyers escape from Europe. He was shipped by train with one thousand prisoners from France to Buchenwald, a concentration camp. "Next to my faith in God," he said, "it was my constant anger at the Nazis for having deprived me of my liberty and their inhuman treatment of their prisoners that stimulated my determination to survive and to deny them the satisfaction of seeing me die."[2]

Dr. Baars explained that he could not show his anger outwardly without meeting certain death at the hands of his captors. He experienced his feelings of anger as *energy* to keep himself alive, while others succumbed to apathy and despair. Having lost their will to live, they died from minor illnesses and infectious diseases. In the end, only six of the original one thousand prisoners survived the ordeal.

This story shows how valuable our feelings are to us and how some of our feelings, though they have important behavioral functions, are still free in relation to these functions.

Feelings, whatever kind they are, emerge in the feminine side of our spontaneous self. As these feelings lead to impulses, and impulses to actions, we move into the masculine side of our spontaneous self; we tend to act as we feel. Some of our spontaneous actions are good for us and others are harmful. Another part of our feminine-masculine self is called upon to discriminate between good and harmful spontaneous actions. This part of our self, our responsible self, takes care of our spontaneity.

Our Responsible Self

If we say to ourselves, "Don't feel angry because you might make the wrong choice and do the wrong thing," or "Feel this!" or "Don't feel that!" we are telling our feelings what to *do*. This is a harmful way of trying to take care of our spontaneous self. Feelings need to be spontaneous; they need to *be,* not *do.* And we need to let them be what they are no matter how pleasant or unpleasant.

127

Responsibility begins in receptivity. We take care of our feelings by receiving them. Received feelings are given a chance to grow as feelings—as energy for be-ing, not just as energy for doing. Then we grow as persons who are sensitive, aware of what we feel, and able to share ourselves in our relationships.

Received feelings also leave us free to act or not to act. They leave us free to listen to the call of our being for integrity in our actions. We receive our values as well as our feelings, and these values help us guide our behavior.

While the feminine side of our responsible self receives our feelings and values, the action-impulses from our feelings call for the attention of the masculine side of our responsible self. With the help of this masculine awareness we watch over our action-impulses. We are as firm with our impulses as we are affirming with our feelings. And we firmly guide our behavior according to our values.

Some of our impulses lead to inner actions such as decisions and choices. These impulses, too, need our masculine watchfulness and guidance.

For example, anger is a spontaneous feeling, and is good as such. But anger can lead to hatred, vengeful decisions, and destructive actions. Vengeance is a feeling of anger that is elaborated by the will, and is not simple, original, spontaneity of feeling. Decisively adulterous desire, too, is a bad action of the mind and will, and involves more than our original sexual feelings.

If we abdicate our responsibility for our impulses and decisions about them, we soon find ourselves saying, "Do whatever you feel." But this is just as bad for our feelings as it is for our actions.

In learning how to take care of our feelings and behavior, we need a clear awareness of the difference between feeling and acting. If we say to ourselves, "Don't have sexual feelings because you might act inappropriately," we identify our feelings and behavior too closely. We are then inclined to impose our values on our feelings like a perfectionist, or else to derive our values from our feelings like a permissive selfist. We need more

128

room, more resting space, between feeling and acting. This inner space is impossible to find without receptivity.

Our Integrative Awareness

Both the spontaneous and responsible parts of our self need our awareness. When we do not know what our feelings are, or how to take care of them in relation to our behavior, these parts of our self are like two people groping around in the dark. They relate in a helter-skelter fashion, or they cling to each other, or they keep their distance. They simply do not know how to relate.

Awareness is the light that lets us see both parts of our life, as well as letting them "see" each other. Awareness gives them the chance they need to learn how to live together in harmony without impulsion or compulsion.

Awareness is initially receptive, then subsequently discerning. Receptive awareness lets the truth reveal itself even when it hurts. Truth about oneself that hurts makes people want to avoid awareness. Then they abandon all hope for inner integration.

The receptive kind of awareness does not *look at* things simply as objects. More than acting like a searchlight looking for an object, the receptive mind acts like a floodlight; it fills "the whole room" with light and *lets* whatever is there *reveal itself.*

We can begin to turn on the light by becoming honestly aware of our spontaneous self. "Am I spontaneously more loving than selfish or more selfish than loving, or about equally both?" This is not a question about behavior, nor even about decisions. While love and selfishness can include decisions we make, both qualities have a feeling-component: an instant response to a situation that happens before we have time to think. How do we immediately tend to respond?

The following scale might be helpful:

loving   a   b   c   d   e   selfish

If we are almost completely loving, we circle the a; almost completely selfish: e; more loving than selfish: b; more selfish than loving: d; and about equally loving and selfish: c. Let us not circle what we think we should or would like to be, but what we honestly perceive we are.

Then we can try to become aware, using a scale from a to e, of other feelings we experience such as joyful/sad, compassionate/indifferent, courageous/ afraid, cheerful/depressed, energetic/lazy, interested/uninterested, amiable/angry. None of these feelings are bad as such, not even selfish feelings. They are just true.

If we notice that the pattern of our spontaneous life tends more toward the negative side of the scale, or more toward d and e, the responsible part of our self might wonder about our attitudes. Negative attitudes such as suspicion and pessimism tend to pull our emotional life toward the negative side of the scale. "Am I suspicious, cynical, pessimistic, or generally negative?" If the answer to any of these is yes, the responsible part of our self can then change our attitude(s), and indirectly move our spontaneous self toward the positive side of the scale.

Next we can become aware of the different kinds of spontaneity in ourselves. One kind *precedes* responsibility: "I feel loving when someone cares for my needs." Another kind of spontaneous feeling *motivates* responsibility: "When I feel loving toward my friends, I want to help them with their problems." And another *results from* responsibility: "When I feel lazy and selfish and go to work anyway, *I feel good* about doing my best in spite of it all."

Finally, a sharpened awareness of our responsible self lets us know when we are compulsive perfectionists: "When it's time for dinner, I have my big meal even if I don't feel like eating." Awareness also lets us know when we are permissive: "I eat only when I feel like it; mostly hamburgers, fries and ice cream." And we can know, too, when we are genuinely responsible. (The next section of this chapter explains and shows how.)

130

Our integrative awareness brings our spontaneous and responsible selves together in harmony. As a result, we can become responsibly spontaneous, and spontaneously responsible.

The integrating process begins as we receive our being: our deepest and most important responsibility. *While our most basic, our integrative, self receives our being, our responsible self (as such) receives the feelings and values that come from our being.* In other words, the integrative self *is* both spontaneous and responsible *in its own way.* It is then able to clarify and harmonize the spontaneous and responsible parts of the self.

By receiving being, our integrative awareness also receives the tendency of being toward doing. Our feminine power for *receiving* leads to our masculine power for *expressing* what is received. Reciprocally, our expressions (our actions) strengthen, develop, and complete our being.

In this reciprocal sense, the feminine and masculine come from each other. They liberate and fulfill each other. They integrate. Like a woman and man in a healthy marriage, who have a healthy ability to care for children, these feminine and masculine powers within us can become responsible for the spontaneous.

Because puritanism lacks the feminine in relation to the masculine, it necessarily lacks a healthy relation of the responsible to the spontaneous. The answer to puritanism is, then, the receiving-expressing (af-firming) power of the integrative part of the self.

Receptive awareness gives us the freedom to express or not to express what is received. This freedom gives us the space we need for developing our emotional life. Then we can relate as affirming persons, not just as performing individuals. Sharing (in this way) who we are, we become ready to *cooperate* when we work together.

How to be Spontaneous Responsibly

When we are shopping for groceries, our impulses try to tell us, "If it looks good and tastes good, it *is* good; buy it." But many attractive foods are processed so much they no longer have the vitamins and minerals we need. They are overloaded, instead, with sugar and salt.

By receiving the situation, by taking some time to become *aware* of nutritional values, and by guiding our actions according to these values (thus involving our responsible self), we grow beyond the impulsive child within us. This does not mean that we have to turn off our spontaneous desire for what looks and tastes delicious. We can have food that is high in nutritional value, and that looks and tastes good, too, but in a more wholesome way.

Stopping to think and to learn does not mean we have to abandon our spontaneous self. We would lose our spontaneity only if we got so obsessed with good nutrition we would not care how our food looks and tastes. The responsible part of our self would become compulsive, the opposite extreme from permitting the spontaneous part to become impulsive.

An impulsive person does not stop and think receptively. He or she lacks responsible discipline. A compulsive person makes too much of discipline and gets puritanical about self-control. But a spontaneous person uses discipline to increase spontaneity.

Spontaneity and discipline might seem like opposites we cannot get together. How can we be spontaneous and disciplined at the same time? Even more amazing, how can we use discipline to increase spontaneity?

Members of an orchestra who discipline themselves by practicing for hours can play the music not only correctly, but also spontaneously. They can even sound inspired. But others, who are not disciplined, impulsively make mistakes and spoil the music. Still others get compulsive about correct notes and techniques. These lack all spontaneity and sound boring.

As we become more aware of the relationship between the spontaneous and responsible parts of our self, we realize that spontaneity belongs primarily to our feelings, and discipline belongs primarily to our behavior. We also realize that discipline in our behavior has a beneficial effect on our emotional life. Our feelings need our values, and our values need our feelings. The big question is: how do these two relate well with each other so that we do not succumb to the puritan or playboy influences that haunt our culture?

If enough of us learn how to live well with our feelings and emotions (something neither the puritan nor playboy can do), the character of our culture can move toward more balance and wholeness. Though it cannot be easy at first, it is possible to find this better, much happier way.

CHAPTER ELEVEN

A TRUE SEXUAL REVOLUTION

Our sexuality, above all, involves who we are, then only what we do; it involves our capacity for *being* love, then only our capacity for making love. When we discover that being love, not making love, is the main reason why we have sexual feelings, and when we learn how to live well with these feelings, a true sexual revolution can begin.

The main reason why we have sexual feelings of any kind, no matter what causes them, is that they are a valuable source of energy for developing our manhood and womanhood: our sexuality. They are not just for genital purposes of having sex and having children. Genital sex and its love-giving and life-giving activities, important as they are, are not the main purpose for our sexuality. Seeing this point, and affirming it, is truly revolutionary.

Such a declaration is almost like Copernicus announcing that the sun does not move around the earth, no matter how obviously it appears to do just that. He said that the rotating earth moves, instead, around the sun, and that the sun, not the earth, is the center of the solar system. How were people supposed to accept such news when their experience seemed to tell them the opposite? They must have felt like saying, "Look and see for yourself; the sun is obviously moving around the earth. The earth is clearly the center of the universe."

In a similar way, it seems perfectly obvious that our sexuality is centered in genital sex. Actually, it is centered in our feminine-masculine capacity for the affirming kind of love. Genital sex is not the central reason for our sexual feelings no matter how much it looks or feels that way.

Our sexual feelings are meant, first of all, to stimulate our main sexual organ, the brain, and to make us think about who we are. These feelings are directed toward inward being long before they are ready to be directed toward outward action. These feelings move our heart and make us more sensitive and compassionate. They grow as feelings. They become mature. They become ready for emotional intimacy as an end in itself, without necessarily leading to genital intimacy.

A too-masculine mentality does not understand the value of *being* our manhood or womanhood, or of thinking about who we are and patiently letting our feelings mature before we act them out. This too-masculine mentality does not realize that sexual feelings need to grow well as feelings, otherwise our sexuality is short-circuited by premature activity, and remains undeveloped. And we become sexually retarded.

Our sexual feelings need the understanding of our mind, the affection of our heart, and the decision of our will, in order to grow in depth and richness as feelings. Conversely, our mind, heart, and will need the energy of our sexual feelings in order to become more perceptive, sensitive, and resolute. Each part needs the others to make it balanced and whole.

We can see this kind of relating in the features of the human face. The right eye gives something valuable not only to the left eye, but also to the nose, mouth, and chin. If the right eye were missing, the rest of the face would be less intact. Each part gives something to all other parts, balancing them and making them whole.

This sharing between parts is what is meant by integration. And sexual integration, the unity of all our inner powers, is made possible by our feminine capacity to receive, and by our masculine capacity to distinguish the parts within the whole.

135

Sexual integration of this kind increases sexual—not just genital—potency and responsiveness.

We do not have to *do* anything about our sexual feelings other than (1) receive them as they are, (2) recognize them as good for us, and (3) welcome them as an inner source of energy for becoming thoughtful, sensitive, loving, resolute, and whole.

This truth about sexual feelings, a truth that women yearn to realize, is the way to a real sexual revolution. If we do not have to do anything about our feelings other than receive them as energy for sexual development, we can be sexually active without genital activity, as well as with it. Our capacity for making love actually receives its best power from our capacity for being love. When men, as well as women, learn what this revolution really means, they want it too.

Sexually Active: Three Ways

There are three ways of being sexually active, not just one. The first way is within our own awareness of our sexual being and our sexual feelings. The second is in emotional and mental intercourse between a man and a woman. The third is in genital intercourse and procreation.

The first, the inner way, is central and the most important. The other two ways depend for their wholeness and fulfillment on the first way.

Because we always act, in whatever we do, as a woman or man, we are sexually active in everything we do. This being-centered activity of our womanhood and manhood helps us to realize that our sexual feelings are oriented toward being, then only toward doing.

Sexual activity of the first kind also means that we receive our feelings as energy for *being* love. This does not mean that we arouse our feelings whenever we have them. Nor does it mean masturbation of any kind, including self-arousal with the mind.

136

An active, receptive, awareness of sexual feelings that helps us grow as a loving man or woman simply appreciates these feelings as they spontaneously happen without increasing them any further. Full arousal of erotic and genital feelings is appropriate only to the third way of being sexually active—genital intercourse—in a lifelong commitment.

On the surface of the matter, the above view of arousal might seem puritan in its limitations. However, the puritan did not recognize three ways of being sexually active any more than the playboy now does. These three ways show that the apparent limitations are not really limits, but protectors of an unlimited potential, and guides toward an unlimited growth in our sexual being and personhood.

The First Way

We become sexually active in the first way by receiving our womanhood or manhood with gratitude and by letting our sexuality be active in everything we do. We also move from being to feelings in an af-firming way.

Affirming our feelings means that we let them be, and we value them as good. We are also firm with our feelings, according to our values, when we do not cause them to grow bigger than they are, and when we restrain the impulses that emerge from these feelings.

Restraint might make us fear repression. But these are two different matters. Restraint is healthy for feelings; repression is unhealthy.

Restraint is needed for the development of love in our feelings. Then we can be loving, as a woman or man, in everything we do.

Repression, on the other hand, has nothing to restrain, and nothing to develop. By repressing our feelings we do not let ourselves feel them consciously, and we do not even let ourselves know that we are repressing. This total absence of receptivity for our feelings is self-destructive.

Unrestrained, and therefore undeveloped, sexual energy is like a child gleefully pounding a piano. Developed sexual energy is like an inspired, disciplined, yet highly spontaneous artist playing the piano. Restraint within spontaneity heightens the artist's creative energy, and makes the music powerful and beautiful.

Another comparison is a current of water in a river. The power of the current, through the proper transforming equipment, can be heightened into electricity for light and warmth in our homes. In a similar way, affirming restraint can heighten the energy of our sexual feelings into warmth in our hearts and light in our minds. Restraint, the firmness within affirmation, thus increases sexual potency.

The organ that transforms sexual "water power" into sexual "electricity" is the brain. Once activated by the affirming mind, this massive generator is able to heighten sexual feelings into the light of awareness and the warmth of love.

The transformed energy that results is, paradoxically, both tranquil and intense. This energy can relax; it can also become passionate. We can relax our feelings by affirming them, or we can intensify our feelings toward the third way.

The first way is the heart of true sexual freedom. Our ability to receive our feelings as energy for *being* love without having to act out our feelings gives us the power to make love without necessity; without impulsion or compulsion. We are able to choose or not to choose the genital expression of our feelings. This expression is not regarded, then, as a necessity for sexual wholeness. A person can remain celibate for life and still be a whole, healthy, passionate man or woman.

The playboy notion that sex is necessary or you will get sick is a helpless, impotent view that promotes impulsiveness, not at all the same as passion. A charming child impulsively "playing the piano" is quite different from a passionate musician who can hear the music in silence as well as in performance.

The first way, centered in the brain and heart (the "heart" is the feeling part of the brain), is not the same in women and men. The first kind of sexual activity is not neuter. It is sexually nuanced (as described in chapter three). Affirming feelings and restraining impulses has a feminine emphasis in most women, and a masculine emphasis in most men.

Usually the sex urge is more emotional than genital in females. They feel an especially strong desire for emotional security. This emphasis can make women (especialy when young) clinging and possessive. Women need to receive their emotional feelings with understanding, and they need to restrain their emotional impulses.

The male, on the other hand, is usually more challenged by his physical feelings. He has a special need for receptivity in his self-concept, otherwise his performance impulses can run away with his situation.

The emotional emphasis of desire in the female, and the physical emphasis of desire in the male, both need the integrating power of affirming love. The female calls her emotional desire love, and the male calls his more physical desire love. But love is much more than these kinds of erotic desire.

Because the English language has only one word for the many meanings of love, this word, love, can be very confusing. The Greek language does better by having three words for love: eros, agape, and philia. Eros desires. Agape gives. Philia shares.

Eros (desire) seeks self-fulfillment. It is self-oriented. Agape (giving) is charity toward someone else. It is other-oriented. Philia (sharing) integrates both self and other in the relation of friendship.

The affirming kind of love is different from eros, agape, and philia. It is most like agape, however, because it gives. But agape and affirmation are different ways of giving.

Agape gives directly to the other, and *does* good for the other. Affirming love gives mainly by receiving, and is not basically concerned about doing. Affirming love says, "I receive the goodness of your being, and I respond, not so much by giving *myself* to you, as by giving *you* to yourself. I receive and give, not so much in my actions, as in my being, my heart. And I let you know my response by my spontaneous enjoyment of your presence." Affirmation does not hide spontaneity.

Affirming love is the heart of eros, agape, and philia. Eros without affirmation is sheer possessiveness. Agape without affirmation is "busy about many things" for the sake of others. Philia without affirmation is just a functional kind of sharing (like playing tennis together), and does not really get into the intimacy of friendship.

The first way of being sexually active unites the feminine and masculine sides of our sexuality in the affirming and firming sides of affirmation. True sexual freedom results. The being of love then leads to expression in the other kinds of love. As a result, sharing, giving, and desiring can become integrated and whole.

The Second Way

The second way of being sexually active follows from the first. *Within* leads to *with*.

When we learn the first way in relation to our own feelings, we discover that we want emotional intimacy in our relationships more than we want sex. We want to receive and give emotional warmth. We want to share mutual support and understanding. We want to talk and listen. The second way is an emotional and mental kind of sexual intercourse. The heart and brain (sexually different in women and men) are the organs for this intercourse.

Man-woman friendship (philia) develops in the second way. Eros might grow within the context of friendship. (Eros should not grow without it.) But the fullness of eros is reserved for the third way.

Friendship combines affirming love with liking. Friends feel a special kind of emotional and mental affection for each other. They also experience mutual esteem, equality, and value-sharing. These three qualities, together with affection, comprise the four qualities of friendship, all of which are completed by the power of affirming love.

In man-woman sharing, the four qualities of friendship are not neuter, but are involved in the sexual intercourse of talking and listening, as well as in other activities. Doing something together in charity toward others can be a co-creative kind of sexual intercourse.

Though second-way intercourse does not have to lead any further, this co-creative kind prepares for the third way's procreative kind. A man and woman need to learn to care for others before they are ready to care for their own children.

Second-way intercourse is physically warm and intimate, but not in the same way as third-way intercourse. Friendship includes second-way touching and holding. A man and woman who are sexually active in the first way can warmly touch and hold each other without arousing erotic desire. They learn the real, and very important, difference between the affirming touch and the arousing touch.

The touch that receives and gives being is basically different from the touch that desires. The desiring touch needs the affirming touch as much as a smile needs a face. But the desiring touch emerges within the affirming touch only if time and deep patience have developed, first, the affirming touch.[1]

The Third Way

Finally, the third way of being sexually active is physical-emotional arousal and genital intercourse: the usual meaning for the phrase "sexually active." It is the most obvious and easiest meaning to understand. But it is not the primary meaning.

Our sexuality needs to be developed throughout our personality by the first and second kinds of sexual activity before we are ready for marriage and genital intimacy.

This process of sexual development is like climbing a mountain. We start at the bottom. We have to struggle to find our way. But if we want to enjoy the climb, we need to take our time. We can learn many things about ourselves, our partner, and the mountain.

Only after we get to the top, after all that climbing, struggling, sharing, enjoying, exercise, and learning, are we ready for the genital expression of our sexuality. Then it is really a peak experience.

But many wonder what they are supposed to do with their strong desire to make love when they have these feelings. What does a mountain climber do with his or her desire to be at the top while still at the bottom? The power of desire is supposed to generate the energy needed to reach the peak.

If we do not take the time to go through this development first, we are like the individual who tries to swim in a pool before filling it with water. If there is no water, we cannot swim. If there is not enough water, we swim with difficulty or not at all.

If the water is deep enough, however, it buoys us up and we can swim with much more freedom and enjoyment. In other words, the "inner pool" of our sexuality needs some *depth* of development before it can buoy us up for a happy experience of marriage and genital intimacy.

Genital intercourse has two important, and equal, purposes. When it emerges out of its needed context, it expresses marital love between a man and woman, and it is able to begin the life of a child. Genital intercourse is love-giving and life-giving.

Most acts of genital intercourse in a relationship are love-giving without starting a new life. Most take place in the infertile phase of the woman's fertility cycles. These acts are designed to be *functionally* love-giving even if they are not *functionally* life-giving. Yet they are designed *always* to be *naturally* both love-giving and life-giving.

The clear difference in the *quantity* of love-giving and life-giving acts might seem to affect their *quality*, and lessen their equality. But number does not affect value. The two purposes of genital intercourse are equal in value.

Equality, however, does not mean sameness. Love-giving and life-giving are different values. We might call the first a general value, and the second a specific value.

Expressing love is a general value of genital sex because there are so many other ways of expressing sexual love besides genital intercourse, such as sharing a meal together. Starting a new life is the one specific value of genital sex because there is no other way of producing the sex-cells that cause new life. (Even if a child is conceived in a dish by domination technology, the mutual causes of the conception are taken from the genital organs of a woman and man.)

Something similar to the general and specific purposes of genital sex would be the two purposes of our sense of sight. There is no other way to see except with our eyes. Seeing, then, is the specific purpose of our sense of sight. But seeing is not the only purpose for our eyes. Looking into another person's eyes, while it involves seeing, can be also a way of expressing love. Or doubt or anger or rejection.

Genital acts can take place, of course, without any love-giving or life-giving feelings at all. Such acts are little more than biological events of copulation and generation, linked, perhaps, with indifference or hatred. Rapists and prostitutes can perform these acts without their appropriate emotional feelings.

Even when genital intercourse does not begin the life of a child, its love-giving emotion tends to include the life-giving emotion in sexually integrated people. This parental feeling can be related to a child the couple hopes to conceive sometime in the future, or to a child or children they already have.

Love-giving and life-giving emotions develop initially in the first and second ways of being sexually active. Without considerable personal growth in these ways, genital intimacy is premature.

When love-giving and life-giving feelings are developed enough to complete their *genital* sexuality, a man and woman might choose to give themselves to each other for life. They are ready to become spouses and parents.

But many people ask, "Why marriage?"

143

The *specific* purpose of genital sex shows that a child is a lasting bond of both parents. The child is symbolically two in one flesh, while being personally his or her own unique flesh. The child needs physical, emotional, mental, and spiritual parenting. And continuity of all these dimensions with the genetic is the most integrating.

The specific purpose of genital sex calls for a stable and lasting bonding of the parents. True sexual potency and responsiveness in the couple is sensitive enough to recognize, affirm, and determine to live, this call.

Marriage is also required by the total nature of genital sexuality. Genital intercourse is a union of persons, not just a union of their bodies. This act expresses a union of persons almost as intimate as each person's union with him or her self. If each of us can live with our own self *for life,* we can live with one other person of the opposite sex for life. Sexuality and personhood are so intimate.

Marriage, however, does not necessarily complete genital sexuality. Marriage, too, can be premature. It can take place before the two people develop their sexuality, and before the love-giving and life-giving emotions are sufficiently mature.

The "mountain" within our sexuality must be climbed. We start at the bottom and gradually move upward toward the peak. Otherwise we frustrate our sexual development.[2]

In summary, we need to find the center between the suppressed and repressed sexuality of the puritan culture on the one side, and the impulsive sexuality of the playboy culture on the other side. This center is the power in our being for affirming love. We develop this power in the first way of being sexually active. From this first way, affirming love extends into the second and third ways.

Finding the *center* ("the sun") of our sexuality, and living within and from this center as whole women and whole men, is the meaning of the true sexual revolution.

Neither the puritan nor the playboy, as such, can find and live this better way. If we find the feminine, the receptive, side of ourselves, which they lack, we can move beyond their

144

spiritual and sexual helplessness toward greater balance and wholeness. For this kind of movement in our culture, we need a better awakening—a new awareness—in the keepers of the feminine.

CHAPTER TWELVE

WHAT WOMEN REALLY WANT

Sigmund Freud's question, "What does a woman want?" must be answered by each individual woman. But women need plenty of awareness before they can answer this question wisely. Without a raising and deepening of awareness, there is too much danger that a woman will slip into a masculine way of thinking about herself. If she has not learned how to think in a woman's way, what defense does she have against the masculine civilization that surrounds and penetrates her? How is she even able to give an intelligent answer to Freud's question?

Becoming personal for a moment, when I studied philosophy in both undergraduate and graduate schools, the term "women's liberation" was not yet heard. But I was quite aware of being in a man's world where no woman philosopher was studied, or, for that matter, had any effect at all on the mind that built Western civilization. I was aware of the feminine aspect of my own mind, and of the absence of the feminine in the philosophers we studied. This awareness saved me from developing my mind in the male mold.

Basically, I related with the great male minds of history in a woman's way, and did not think I had to master their way of thinking. The result was a tremendous experience in creative thinking, and a very exciting discovery of a different kind of wisdom. My own mental fertility could have been disturbed or even ruined by the all-male way of thinking. By relating with the philosophers as a woman, not by adopting their frame of mind, I experienced a woman's liberation.

As for answering Freud's question, I would say, after learning from life and pondering the matter, that women want awareness, wholeness, and sharing. (These qualities are based on the emphasis generally found in the female organization of the brain: *knowing* versus thinking and the *integration* and *relationship* between brain hemispheres.) Women want many other things, too, of course, but basically they want their choices to be wise, integrated, and loving. In this way, they can find an authentic liberation.

Women Want Awareness

By developing their own kind of awareness within their own being, women can begin the process of transforming civilization. A woman's good effect on the world must begin *within* herself. If it does not begin within, it cannot begin at all.

If women really want to begin changing the too-masculine character of civilization, one of the best places to start is where the masculine mentality most despises the human person in our time: in the fertility of the person's body.

Women who insist that the *fertility of persons* is a healthy part of male and female personhood, and who demand respect for this despised part of themselves, can start the needed revolution. These women are able to change the mentality that forms our masculine way of thinking and living.

Though the courts of the land have protected women from awareness of the growing little person within a mother's body, and though many male-dominated women accept, and even defend, this "protection," women really do want to know. They do not want the male mind to prevent them from knowing the whole truth.

This whole truth will affect the decisions women make. Women want Constitutional rights and protection, but they do not really want to make choices with Constitutionally protected ignorance about all that is involved in their choices. Who wants such belittlement?

And though the extremely masculine concept of birth control (birth-domination) induces many women to manage their fertility in a male-dominated way, they really want to regulate their fertility by knowing their fertility. They honor their minds and their bodies enough to want such awareness and self-regulation.

Human fertility, like a child, needs watchfulness. The responsible part of the self, like a healthy parent, neither encroaches on fertility nor becomes permissive. Fertility cycles are allowed to be what they are, but they are not allowed to go unattended. The power to begin new life is neither tyrannized nor abandoned.

The responsible part of the self, like a healthy inner parent, integrates fertility awareness into sexual awareness. This requires feminine receptivity, the integrating power. The responsible part of the self regulates fertility by learning its cycles and regulating sexual expression. *Such integration requires true sexual potency and responsiveness:* holistically sexual, not just genital, competence.

Many men, especially those who are too performance-oriented, do not want to wait around long enough for a woman to grow in mind-body-fertility awareness. Such a receiving kind of awareness takes time. *Being* always takes time even when *doing* gets impatient. Whole women take that time receptively and assertively. And they realize that only whole men are potent enough to cooperate with them.

Women want the full male potency of whole men who develop their own male receptivity. But how can women expect this of men if women do not develop their own receptivity, especially their receptivity for the natural bond of sex with fertility? A woman who says, "I want to control my body by knowing my body, and by af-firming my wholeness in intercourse with you" delivers a challenging invitation to the puritan and/or playboy that might be lurking in a man.

Whole women want the awareness they need to regulate their fertility in a woman's way. Men who integrate the feminine side of themselves, who become whole men, want to receive and respect the woman's way. They want to integrate the woman's way into the man's way, and vice versa. They want women to have mind-body-fertility awareness. And they want to cooperate with a woman by regulating their own performance-impulses.

There is much more to the fertility of persons than biological fertility. There is also mental and emotional fertility (resourcefulness), just as there is mental and emotional sexuality.

Respect for biological fertility increases emotional and mental fertility. The couple learns how to express sexual feelings in more ways than one. Masculine methods of birth control, because they separate what should remain intact, detract from emotional and mental fertility, and also foster sexual impulsiveness. The result can be a kind of sexual impotence and frigidity.

The fertility awareness required by natural family planning necessarily expands into other kinds of awareness as well. Sexuality awareness is challenged to grow.

Fertility awareness and regulation calls for man-woman sharing at the precise point where men tend to abandon women. Men try to make women responsible either by letting women bear all possible children, or by supplying women with the too-masculine "tools" of birth control.

But male fertility is deeply involved with female fertility. Consequently, the male mind should be deeply involved with the female mind in developing the fine art of fertility awareness and conception regulation.

Together they *receive* and *parent* their shared fertility. Their responsibility takes care of their spontaneity. By learning how to parent their fertility, the two learn the parenting art in a way that prepares them for having children. They develop care for a challenging kind of spontaneity that needs constant responsible attention.

Parents who cannot, or will not, regulate their sexuality send out a nonverbal message to their children that no words or actions can silence. Contraception and sterilization say "impulsive sex" to everyone, no matter what else is said or done. And children are especially quick to get the message.

Fertility regulation (the fine art way) means fertility integration, not suppression. Nor repression. Integrating methods help the process of sexual integration within each of the two persons. These methods are a crucial test for the wholeness of a woman and the wholeness of a man; and for the wholeness of their relationship. Women who want awareness, wholeness, and sharing insist—and will insist more and more—that this test be passed.

And when the test is passed, birth controlling drugs, devices, and surgeries of all kinds will not be able to survive the power of a woman's true self-awareness. A new women's movement can change profoundly the effect that women are having on human relationships, and on the mentality that forms our culture.

As long as most women remain unaware of the totally masculine character of birth control by the domineering methods of contraception, sterilization, and abortion, and of the masculine domination of their minds about this subject, the keepers of the feminine will have abandoned their mission at that precise point where they can make a real difference. If women fail, here, to change the prevailing puritan-playboy mentality, they will fail also on the level of culture and civilization.

If women cannot find sexual integration in the flesh-and-blood connection between sexuality and fertility, if they cannot release the integrating power of receptivity precisely here, they bring a kind of hypocrisy into the other dimensions of life, and can have no profound and lasting effect. The awareness women really want is that sensitive, and that responsive.

Women Want Wholeness

Women, not men, were the ones who started a revolution against separate, stereotypical roles for the sexes. Deep down in themselves, men really want this revolution. But we would be waiting yet for men to start it.

Men can live without wholeness more easily than women. Women want to integrate the masculine side of themselves in their own feminine way before men want to integrate the feminine side of themselves in their own masculine way. Men are still resisting their own unique receptivity. As long as they do so, they will continue to be either puritans, or playboys, or both together in an unintegrated way.

When a man recognizes and integrates the feminine side of himself, he is more at home with himself. He then feels more at home with women, and is able to *be with* them, and share feelings with them. He is not afraid of friendship and emotional intimacy with a woman. He does not feel impelled to prove he is a man by using a woman to glorify himself.

When a woman recognizes and integrates the masculine side of herself, she is able to be herself in peace, no matter what tactics or strategies puritans and playboys use to make her serve their self-justification. She is able to affirm men, *be with* them, and call them to their own kind of wholeness. This mutual integration within, and between, women and men is the kind of wholeness women really want.

Men who integrate the receptive side of themselves do not, for that reason, become "women." They become more fully men, gentle and tough at once. They develop the sexual potency of whole men, not just the performance potency of all-male, half-men. Women, too, give up the all-female, half-woman status of the feminine mystique, and become more fully women.

Women can invite, and even challenge, men to develop their own male receptivity, and, as a result, their full male potency. Men do not want the female kind of receptivity, and should not be pressured. The most significant indication of a man's receptivity, and also of his sexual potency, is his ability to *receive* his genital sexuality, and to free his urges from *necessary* expression. This kind of sexual freedom—the height of male potency—is, at present, quite unthinkable to most men. It will require the masculine qualities of strength and courage for men to develop receptivity in their performance sexuality.

Can women really lead men to their own (their male) kind of receptivity?

Women can let men know that they *value* a man's receptivity as much as they value his action-orientation. Women can nurture receptivity in men. They can encourage silence, stillness, and contemplation at times. No "how to" chapter or book can tell a woman how to "water the roots" in her own unique situation. The "watering power" of awareness is already a good beginning. Even a beginning of receptivity in a man gives him *power* to grow in true sexual freedom: his access to the friendship whole women desire to share with whole men.

As long as relationships *necessarily* gravitate toward the bedroom, we are not sexually free enough for friendship. Though friends can become lovers, they do not *have to* do so. This freedom of heart and mind is necessary for the development of friendship as friendship. Otherwise man-woman friendship is short-circuited, and never really has a chance to center in its own potential for happiness.

Men are not likely to begin any kind of movement into human receptivity, true sexual freedom, and the new holistic sexuality. Most of them seem unaware of their absent receptivity, and can live without it, as long as women passively accept the situation. Once women increase the needed awareness, however, and once men catch on and experience the joy of the benefits, they will probably surprise women with their initiative. The original leader might become, also, a grateful follower.

Beyond the half-person condition of performance sexuality, woman and man, hand in hand, mind in mind, can become co-creative friends.

They can receive together their call to wholeness within their very human brokenness. They can climb the inner mountain

152

together. But they need more than a masculine way of thinking to understand their sharing of wholeness.

While Anne Wilson Schaef, the author of *Women's Reality,* says many insightful things about a woman's gender uniqueness, she uses a masculine way of interpreting the human situation. She thinks that a woman's way of coming to wholeness is to leave what she calls the Female System and to go into the Male System by doing things the male's way, then by going back into the Female System. She says, "It seems as if we must first be successful in the White Male System before we can fully and with clarity move into the Female System." [1] She sees the male and female systems as separate realities, and women moving out of one half-system into another and back again.

A more feminine way of thinking would see women bringing their feminine awareness into the male system, transforming the male system into a greater human wholeness, and finally, deepening and expanding the union of male and female in one whole system.

Schaef says that people from the two systems, male and female, can truly begin to relate and connect only when both are willing to recognize and understand each other's systems. But this means connecting from the outside. The two systems remain separate as they reach out to touch each other.

A more feminine way of thinking would begin with a greater sense of continuity and intimacy between feminine and masculine. A feminine view would begin with a vision of one balanced system instead of two separate systems trying, too often unsuccessfully, to get along with each other.

The feminine side of the mind is the source of continuity between feminine and masculine. This is true in both women and men. They can understand that each has something of the other within themselves. They can *discover* the unity and relationship that already exists between them, rather than trying to *impose* this unity upon a more basic disjunction.

Coming to wholeness requires receptivity. There is no wholeness without it. Receptivity is the beginning and continuous source of wholeness.

We need to begin by receiving the gift of being. This happens, most often, in silence and contemplation.

Anne Morrow Lindbergh, in her beautiful book, *Gift from the Sea*, shows how silence and contemplation lead to the kind of wholeness that women want, the wholeness of *being*, and of the kind of activity that emerges from within, and expresses this wholeness.

Her husband, Charles Lindbergh, was an extremely independent, competent, and scientifically logical person. Anne shared many of his flying ventures. She became a skilled navigator and radio operator as they surveyed air routes around the world. Years of sharing softened Lindbergh's perceptions.

By the spring of 1942, he was sensitive enough to write Anne a letter that showed how much she had changed his life: "Largely through you I have touched and glimpsed something so much greater than this world of industrial power and whirring efficiency that all this fades into unimportance in comparison."[2] Even Charles Lindbergh, an individualist and achiever of the highest male order, sensed the great importance of the receptive (feminine) sense of being.

Women Want Sharing

Friendship between the feminine and masculine sides of life—not separation, conflict, and truces—is the deepest desire of a woman's heart. Friendship is a sharing kind of love. A man and woman who know how to share, not just the things they *do* together, but *who they are* (their feelings, meanings, and values), are able to be friends.

Women want to share achievements with men. But this is not enough. Individualists tend to share their work and objective interests, not themselves. Often, men are satisfied with this kind of sharing. Women want persons to share themselves, and only then their work and other interests.

Intimacy comes first, then efficiency. The kind of intimacy women most deeply want, however, is not just another kind of performance. It is a verbal sharing that comes from the heart (the heart of the mind, and the mind of the heart). It is talking and listening from *within*.

The big problem here is that many men do not *like* to listen. Listening is receptive. It is not just the toleration of waiting for someone else to finish talking so you can take your turn to talk. It is not physical presence along with mental or emotional absence. The best listeners listen with their feelings as well as their awareness. To listen this way, we have to value our ability to feel and to empathize with someone else.

Besides having a problem with listening as such, many men do not like to listen to women talk. They don't like what women talk about, and what seems to them the illogical way they talk. Besides, they think women talk too much.

In his book, *The Gift of Feeling,* Paul Tournier sympathizes with women. "Do you not think that the reason why women talk so much is that men hardly ever listen to them? It is a vicious circle: the more silent the man is, the more the woman talks, and the more she talks, the more silent he remains. As a result of having to talk in a void, the woman comes to take her own words less seriously, and her talk turns into aimless chatter." [3]

The reason why some men do not like to listen to women is that they do not *like* women as female persons. They *like* women as objects, and they *love* women as their mothers, sisters, and wives. But *liking* women *as women?* That is something quite different.

Because friendship is not possible without liking, friendship of men toward women is a special challenge. If men were more inclined to *like* their own receptivity, the situation could change more easily. But many fear receptivity. They avoid it. They prefer to be half-men. They have a hard time feeling at home with themselves.

Consequently, the person-to-person sharing that is such an intimate, receptive, part of friendship is difficult for many men, and is not a high priority for them. One writer on the topic, Daniel Levinson, says of his study of men, that friendship is noticeable by its absence, and that close friendships are rarely experienced by American men. He says that a man may have many "friendly" relationships with other men and a few women, but that most men do not have intimate male friends nor an intimate non-sexual (non-genital) friendship with a woman. [4] There must be a significant reason why intimate friendship is such a rare experience for men.

Writing about the difference between closed and open men, Steven Naifeh and Gregory Smith in their book, *Why Can't Men Open Up?* say "Men must reject, suppress, or ignore their feelings, and search instead for the appropriate response. A man cannot ask himself, 'How do I feel?' He must ask, 'How am I supposed to feel?'"[5]

Anyone who has to ask the question, how am I supposed to feel, is doing with feelings what should not be done. That person probably heard, much too often, "Feel this; don't feel that." But feelings are supposed to be spontaneous; no manhandling allowed. We are supposed to take care of our feelings by letting them be what they are, and by being watchful and firm with their impulses toward action. Saying, "Feel this; don't feel that" is careless and domineering.

Sadly, boys often learn early in life to feel this and not to feel that. In other words, have your masculine feelings, the ones that make you tough and competitive, but don't allow yourself to feel anything that undermines your *control* of the situation. Vulnerability is not allowed. The more receptive feelings, such as compassion and empathy, belong to girls and women, not to men. Girls can feel hurt, cry, and be afraid. Not boys.

Naifeh and Smith put it succinctly. "These are the lessons a young man learns on the playing field, in the movie theater, and on the television screen: to be a man in society means to struggle mightily each day to suppress one's emotions, assert one's independence, cling to one's goals, surpass one's competitors, and the next day, return to begin the struggle again." These

156

authors acknowledge that a man needs such lessons in order to give his family a sense of solidity and security in a competitive world. But they also see the problem: "Even as they make his outer life easier, these lessons of manhood will make his inner life more difficult." [6]

A constricted emotional life militates against sharing and friendship. Some women are narrow and closed emotionally, and some men are more open and spontaneous. Generally, however, it is the woman who longs to get in touch emotionally, and who is deeply disappointed and even shocked to find, in the end, that "there is no one home."

Women can encourage men to listen by asking questions about a man's feelings and personal thoughts, the very things he wants to keep to himself. But he keeps them to himself mostly because he is *unaware* of what he really feels and subconsciously thinks. Men need and want awareness, too.

A woman can encourage a man to become aware of his real self by asking appropriate questions, and by listening with her feelings and awareness to what he says. At first he is likely to answer in terms of what he thinks, knows, and does. But questions should go beyond these into the right side of his brain. What is your earliest memory of another person? When did you first become aware of yourself? You had fun playing ball with Pete and Marty, but what did they mean to you beyond that? You felt embarrassed, didn't you? Isn't that OK?

When he finally feels at home answering questions like these, a man's inner self might wake up and ask a woman similar questions. He might get interested in her real self, and genuinely might want to listen.

Women love talking and listening. They also love touching and holding.

One time, after I gave a talk on the importance of women, a woman said to me, "I wish my husband would just hold me sometimes." To him, touching and holding always meant sex: physical action.

His view is commonplace today. Unfortunately, we live in a culture that discourages touching. Our society tells us that touch

157

means either sex or aggression. So we are afraid to display affection for fear of being misunderstood. The problem is intensified by the growing awareness about sexual abuse of children. Many are afraid to touch other people's children out of fear they might be accused falsely of sex abuse.

Puritanism tied the sense of touch too closely to sex; Victorianism feared sex too much and kept it rigidly in its place. As a result, touching and holding were, and often still are, reserved for the bedroom. People frequently seek sex just to get the touching and holding they need, and also, become quite obsessed with sex. But sex, a different kind of contact, cannot satisfy our more basic need for physical closeness.

Touch-deprived people, besides being more obsessed with sex, are also more prone to violence. They substitute slapping, fighting, raping, and even killing, for the affirming touch.

Hands that touch to heal and comfort express affirmation. The love that passes from one person to another through the sense of touch is calming, life-giving, and healing. It is integrating.

Scientific evidence shows the favorable effects of touch on the human body. Heartbeats stabilize. Palsy victims improve their movements. Children with Down's syndrome walk at an earlier age. Students get higher grades in school. Friendships thrive. Marriages are happier.

Even babies in the womb respond to touch in a remarkable way. Through her sense of touch, a mother can give her baby affirming love before the baby is born. When the woman is about five months pregnant, she can "rock" her baby by putting one hand on each side of her abdomen and simply concentrating her feelings of tender love in one hand and then in the other. The baby moves toward the hand in which the mother's feelings are focused. As the mother "moves her heart" from one hand to the other, the baby moves back and forth to feel her love.[7]

The attitude and touch of affirming love is relaxing, not arousing; it is tender, not erotic. Many parents fail to realize this important difference between the affirming and the arousing touch.

When parents avoid touching their children because they fear sexual implications, their children often have a difficult time with sexual development and have problems with sex later in life. Ironically, parents often cause the very thing they fear (hyperactive sexuality and even homosexuality) by failing to touch and hug their children. Some counselors interpret homosexuality as a result of emotional and touch deprivation by a parent of the same sex, a lack that can cause the child to desire another person of the same sex at a time when erotic feelings are emerging.

The deprivation begins in the relation between a man and woman. They fail to learn, in their own relationship, the difference between the affirming and the arousing touch. Fertility regulation by sexual regulation calls them to this essential growth. Learning the difference between the two kinds of touch, and their connection, is necessary for family wholeness and human happiness.

A man and woman who feel free to touch each other warmly without necessarily getting involved in sex, also feel free to talk and listen, to share their feelings, thoughts, and values. They are able to share who they are. Then their sharing of actions, performances, and achievements is an expression of human wholeness.

CHAPTER THIRTEEN

RESPONSIBLE CHOICE

Women want freedom of choice. They want to choose their own personal path to awareness, wholeness, and sharing. For this purpose, they want their choices to be responsible.

Women really do not want to choose like puritans and playboys, compelled by moralism or impelled by feelings and preferences. They want to find a better way of making choices.

Responsible choice begins in af-firmation. "I receive the goodness of my being; I find in my goodness certain inner requirements for human wholeness; I respond to these requirements with firmness."

Responsible choice, like affirmation, begins in the feminine, the receptive, side of the mind. Receptivity is neither compelled nor impelled; it actually prevents compulsion and impulsion, and increases our freedom to choose. A receiving attitude relaxes us into the goodness of our being before we choose our actions.

Receptivity returns us to the source of our actions. It moves us within, before we move out toward anything else. We choose what to *be* before we choose what to *do*.

Responsible choice affirms our being, the better to be firm with our behavior.

Example: "Here I am pregnant and I really don't want to be. Now is not the time for me to have a child. It would be irresponsible. So I prefer to have an abortion.

"But an abortion goes against my principles; I believe it ends a life. So what can I do? My feelings and my values are in conflict. My preferences and my principles are at odds. If I choose by my feelings and preferences like a selfist, I step into the playboy trap. If I choose by my values and principles *for their own sake,* like a tough individualist, I step into the puritan trap. How can I get beyond this deadlock?"

To Be or Not To Be

Responsible choice is not just a matter of what to do in a situation. It is basically, and most importantly, a matter of what to be. Not "what are my preferences for what to *do,*" or "what are my principles for what to *do?*" But "what kind of person am I going to *be* in my actions?" Person, not preference or principle, is the starting point.

To be a person is to be that kind of being that responds to the awesome reality of being something at all rather than just nothing. A person is one who can respond to being, one who can be response-able. No kind of reality other than a person can be responsible.[1]

The original sin at the bottom of all other sins is a failure to *receive* the gift of being as it is given. The first of all commandments is *be,* and be who you are. Receiving the gift of being is the first of our responsible choices. *Other choices cannot be fully responsible without this one,* whether it is made implicitly or explicitly.

To be or not to be, that is the bottom line. And only the choice *to be* is the responsible one. There is no other alternative for responsibility.

There is another alternative, however. The irresponse-able choice can be just as freely made as the responsible one. Not to respond to being is to be irresponsible, because in choosing not to be, we still *are.* But we *are* in a fallen state. We become the kind of being that "is not" by choice, while continuing to be by substance: a state of disintegration.

161

Such is the great paradox of our freedom. We are most free when we are deciding in the face of two alternatives (no more than that). Whether to be or not to be, whether to receive or not to receive.

The choice *to be* increases our freedom for action. The choice *not to be* decreases our freedom for action.

Whatever our choice about our being, this one choice becomes the fountainhead of our choices about doing. Some action-choices, such as telling the truth, express and strengthen our deeper decision to be. Our speech is integrated with our knowledge. Other action-choices, such as lying, express our decision not to be. Speech and knowledge are disintegrated. Our willingness to receive the gift of being is the first and final test of our freedom and responsibility.

Freedom of choice is not, then, just a matter of increasing our options or expanding our alternatives. Women who think that more options and alternatives for what to *do* is their answer to "the problem that has no name" miss the mark. The nameless problem is centered in a woman's being, and in her call to become a keeper of being and of the relation between being and doing.

To be or not to be has a special significance for women. Eve (the mother of life, and also our power to receive being) was, and still is, the first to say no. She is also the first to say yes. The Eve-power is within women and men, but with a special emphasis in women.

Expanding alternatives for action is the horizontal dimension of freedom. To be or not to be is the vertical dimension. The horizontal needs the vertical, otherwise it falls flat. The vertical is completed in the horizontal just as being is completed in action.

Continuing the example: "I ask myself, 'Who am I in this situation?' I am pregnant and don't want to be. I *am* pregnant. Does this mean that I *am* a mother? If my situation would let me want to be pregnant, I would have no difficulty saying, 'I *am* a mother.' Since I don't want to be a mother, I prefer to say, 'OK, I'm pregnant, but I can terminate my pregnancy.'

"On second thought, is my *situation* telling me whether or not I *am* a mother? Is my wanting or unwanting telling me? Or is my being telling me?

"Why should I let my situation tell me who I am? I am not a passive victim of my situation. Or am I?

"If I am a passive victim of my situation, I can say either of two things, 'I am not a mother and will not give birth,' or 'I am a mother but I won't have this child.'

"But I don't have to be a passive victim of my situation. My being is not my situation. I can be receptive instead of passive.

"Being pregnant, which I definitely am, means I am carrying something. What? It's something that is surely going to make me a mother if I'm not already one. Doesn't that make me a mother in the carrying stage?

"If I deny that I am already a mother, I have to ask myself, 'With what am I pregnant?' If I think I am pregnant with an alien piece of growing tissue, I feel like I'm diminishing myself. Carrying an alien thing like an unwanted tumor belittles pregnancy, and belittles me as one who is able to get pregnant.

"But if I think I am pregnant with another of my own kind, my person and my sexuality immediately have more dignity.

"I suppose I am a mother whether or not I want to be. Just like I am myself whether or not I want to be. If I *am* a mother, I no longer have the freedom to choose whether or not to be a mother. I had that freedom before I became pregnant. But now I'm pregnant and I am a mother in the carrying stage. I can only choose what I am or deny what I am.

"To be or not to be. What kind of mother am I going to be: one who receives my motherhood and gives birth to my child, or one who denies it and removes what I am carrying? If I choose not to be a mother, I remain a mother. The mother of a dead child is still a mother.

"I choose to receive my being as a mother. I choose to receive my situation and to make the best of it somehow. My situation is not going to tell me that I should not be who I am.[2]

"When I receive my situation, this makes my situation a real challenge to my being, no longer just an imposition. I can respond to the challenge according to the kind of person I *really prefer* to be.

"I end up with a different preference than the one with which I started my deliberations. Receptivity deepened my preference. It also brought me into harmony with my principles; not because of my principles, however, but because of my being and the being I am carrying. My principle, 'Do not kill,' is less important to me than my real, living self and my real, living child. But this principle is also important because it nudged me to move beyond my first impulsive preference, and to think about my pregnancy, instead of running to an abortionist to get me out of my being because of my situation.

"My being, my person, led me to my true preference in this situation, and brought together into harmony my preferences and principles. Though I still have some ambivalent feelings, my basic feelings and my values are no longer at odds.

"My first impulsive preference, understandable as it was, is not my final choice. I do not choose according to that impulse because I have received so much more than my first, reacting impulses.

"If it were a matter of choosing which pair of shoes to buy, I would have many alternatives and like it that way. I can always throw away a pair of shoes I do not want, but throwing away my child, even in this carrying stage, is a different matter altogether.

"When I stop to think about the life I am carrying, I realize that a life can *be* before it can *do*. This life within me is in a state of being with no doing to show for it.

"Some people try to tell me that if there is no functional activity, there is no person, no being. But that is an overly masculine (left-brain) way of identifying being with doing.

"The mother experiences the first action of the new life as movement. Then birth. Then crying. This little person cannot do much, cannot talk, walk, take care of feeding and eliminating. Yet the person *is*. Doing is important, in due time, of course. But doing comes out of the being who already is."

Even if a woman does not actually think this way (left brain), she intuits this way (right brain and whole brain). She knows, even if she does not think. And the feminine side of her mind knows all of the above about being, even if the masculine side writes a book (or two or more) against it.

A woman is the kind of person who *can* carry another person within. She need not ever *do* so. But her ability to do so is part of her *being*, and affects her entire self, not just part of herself. Women, in a special way, desire to be valued by others and by themselves just for being who they are. This being-emphasis is, then, of special importance in their choices.

Like a Woman Giving Birth

Responsible choice is like a woman giving birth.

I once talked by phone with a woman whose labor pains were beginning after a very difficult pregnancy. There was reason for her to be afraid. We talked about receptivity. Suddenly she had to leave, and we hung up.

The next morning she called from her hospital bed and said her labor and delivery were short and easy, and that she kept on repeating to herself during that time the word "receive, receive" and practicing it. "It is such a beautiful word," she said.

We deliver our own stages of life, and choose our own actions, often in labor pains. Receptivity can make the process quicker and easier.

A Call to Wholeness and Integrity

As we receive our being, we are given an inner call to wholeness in our person, and to integrity in our actions. Actions that lack integrity undermine wholeness. We are in constant labor and exertion with the challenge of wholeness.

Wholeness means a harmonious relation of parts. Integration means a process of *growing* in wholeness. And integrity means *acting* according to our call to wholeness.

Our values and principles, received from within, not imposed from without, are meant to serve our person, and not the other way around. Persons serve principles in puritan moralism. And persons serve preferences in playboy selfism. Both principles and preferences serve persons in the way of affirmation. Sometimes we may act according to our preferences. At all times, however, our principles guide us in which preferences to follow and which to avoid.

Responsible choice receives both feelings and values (preferences and principles) with equal respect. Received as they are, as related and yet distinct, feelings do not impel, and values do not compel, but leave us free, instead, to choose our actions responsibly. We are then *able* (not helpless) to respond to the call of our being for wholeness and integrity.

Freud and Kohlberg—
Overly Masculine

Sigmund Freud did not think we could receive inner requirements of our person for wholeness and integrity. He lacked an insight into the feminine power to receive these requirements from within. Our social situation, not our inner nature, seemed to be the source of moral guidance. Values had to be imposed from without. People had to be compelled to behave decently.

Alienated from the true source of responsible choice, Freud found himself in the midst of the conflict between preferences and principles. According to his view, society instills the principles that moderate our choices. And he saw these principles as rules, dictates, laws, and all kinds of do's and don'ts.

Eventually, preferences rebelled and buried principles, especially those relating to sexual behavior.

Then Lawrence Kohlberg, an educational psychologist at Harvard University, tried to put principles on top again. He said that we have three levels of motivation, and though many people are motivated by pain and pleasure, the highest and best level is motivation by universal principles, specifically those of justice.

Basing justice on the rights of individuals, Kohlberg reinforced the masculine sense of tough individualism and rational adherence to law. As some feminists later showed, men are more motivated by formal laws and rules than women are.

A Woman Reacts

Carol Gilligan, a professor of education at Harvard, and a student and colleague of Kohlberg, noticed the absence of the feminine in his theory. She reacted by developing three levels of motivation for women, who, she says, are more interested in caring than in justice (*In a Different Voice, 1982*). So now we have two moralities, one for men and their abstract rules, and another for women and their situational cares. The clearly feminist implication is that women do not want to have men's rules imposed on their cares.

In using a masculine logic of identity and separation, Gilligan seems to do little better than Schaef. Both Gilligan and Schaef see life in terms of two systems, one for men and one for women. A more feminine way of thinking would look for the integrating point that unites two different ways of being a person. This point, of course, is the being of the human person, whether woman or man.

There are not two moralities, one for women and one for men.[3] There is only one morality, a morality for all persons as persons. Women and men bring to this single morality different sensitivities and emphases in the decision process. But both are called to the same moral conclusions.

Women really want wholeness, not two different life-systems (Schaef) or two different moralities (Gilligan).

While Gilligan appreciates the different ways in which women and men approach life, she separates, rather than integrates, these differences. Instead of trying to show how the absent feminine perspective in Kohlberg could be integrated into the latter's system, thus changing it profoundly, Gilligan builds another system just as defective as his. Using the abortion decision as her main example, she shows how the formal principles of the male system do not apply to women who are more concerned about responsibility in a particular situation than about universal rules and absolute laws.

Gilligan goes to great lengths to establish abortion as a responsible choice for women. She tries to elevate wanting and unwanting to the highest level of feminine motivation. In other words, she tries to elevate preference over principle for women, just as Kohlberg elevated principle over preference for men.

A woman who says, "I am pregnant and don't want to be, because I *care* for my boyfriend's need to be free of responsibility at this time, for my parent's need to be free of embarrassment and more burdens, for my own need to finish high school, and for the need of a child to be wanted," is revealed by Gilligan as one who really cares and wants to be responsible. This woman's choice to have an abortion, especially if she finally cares about her own needs, can show (thus interpreted) a woman's highest and most mature level of motivation.

According to Gilligan, women are more sensitive than men about care for needs, because they are more centered than men in the self-other relationship. This represents a good, right-brain, emphasis in women. But what happens to the woman's need to receive her own being as a mother, and to her child's need to be received by the mother? Since these latter needs are excluded by the abortion choice, the choice is really based on preferred needs (or on preference) rather than on the person as a person.

By exalting female selfism to the highest level of female motivation, Gilligan really steps into the masculine trap. A woman chooses to assert herself, and to control her own body by forcefully ending her pregnancy. Assertion (balanced masculine) moves into aggression (raw, unbalanced masculine). The woman is now much more like the individualistic and independent male—someone in control—but without his principles of justice.

This likeness to the male appears, in an especially poignant way, in one of the women Gilligan quotes. Talking about the effect that an abortion will have on her emotional life, she says, "Probably what I will do is I will cut off my feelings, and when they will return or what would happen to them after that, I don't know. So that I don't feel anything at all, and I would probably just be very cold and go through it very coldly. The more you do that to yourself, the more difficult it becomes to love again and to trust again or to feel again."[4]

Like the male who hides, ignores, suppresses, or buries his feelings in order to become independent, the aborting woman forces herself to dominate her feelings. How can this be healthy or mature for women?

Failing to begin her critique of Kohlberg by integrating the feminine with the masculine, Gilligan ends up with a masculinized female who is neither feminine in the true sense, nor masculine in the true sense. This female is basically passive to her situation (seeing herself as a victim), and reactive against her situation (trying to control it by aggression). Passivity and reaction, as extremes, are not *responses* (which involve receptivity), and are not truly response-able.

Gilligan's version of responsible choice is also one that could endorse a woman's lack of knowledge as she makes her choice. Were the women in her sample given the information they needed to make a really responsible decision?

Did they listen, with a stethoscope, to the heartbeat of the life within the womb? Did they see a sonogram of the inhabitant? Were they informed about the emotional and physical consequences to themselves, and about alternatives to abortion? Were they encouraged to *think out* what they already *know* about their own being?

With this kind of awareness, a woman could be even more motivated by care. She could then move more readily beyond her initial feelings of passive victimization by her situation, and beyond her first impulsive preferences. The process of making her choice could be more responsible, and not just a rationalized form of irresponsibility.

Where Gilligan sees care as a woman's motivation in not wanting her child, responsible choice extends that care to the child as the deepest and best way for the woman to care for herself. Her need for wholeness and integrity goes deeper than her need for self-centered control and independence.

A Woman Responds

Instead of reacting in the usual feminist way to male sexism, a woman might say to Kohlberg, "I have studied your system of cognitive moral development, and find that a most essential element of all human cognition is missing. You seem to ignore the intuitive (feminine or right brain) kind of knowing.

"Even a small child in the first stages of human development has an intellectually intuitive cognition of *being,* otherwise this child would not be human, but just some kind of sentient organism no different from a cat or dog. The child does not know that he or she knows in this way. The child is not yet aware of this knowing. But neither are you, Professor Kohlberg. You do not appear to be aware that you are knowing *being.* Even though you and the child are not aware of this knowing, it is, nevertheless, a dynamic and motivating part of your cognition, and of your psychological development, including your moral development.

"The right brain knows before we know that we know. And the right brain knows for a good amount of time before the left brain gets involved in any kind of reasoning process, or before we can verbalize what we know. 'I know it but can't say it,' is a common experience. Right-brain cognition is actively present in all our cognitions, and in all our motivations.

"Our intuition of *being* includes a vague, but definite, sense of our call to wholeness and moral integrity. Children have an intuitive sense of good and evil, right and wrong. Since their impulses are not yet guided by their responsible self, these impulses are more immediately motivating until their intuitive awareness is affirmed.

"Instead of trying to motivate children *only* by *training* (via pain and pleasure) their left brain in the principles of behavior, we should try to *nurture* their right-brain intuition. This intuition is directly in touch with what can be formulated later as moral principles.

"The training approach is masculine. The nurturing approach is feminine. Both are needed. But rational training without intuitional nurturing is deadening and not sufficiently motivating. Nurtured intuition naturally leads to reasoning and to an articulation of the person's call to integrity.

"Because of their intuitive emphasis, women do not *need* formalization of principles as much as men do. But the female mind is just as intimately in touch with these real, concrete principles of integrity as the male mind, and is even inclined to articulate them with a feminine emphasis on care-for-self-and-others. Men are more inclined to formulate these same principles, in an abstract way, as universal laws.

"By realizing that the child (male and female) mentally senses the source of moral principles, and the principles themselves, we can nurture this intuition so that it becomes steadily more aware, and steadily more ready for left-brain formulation. We can, in this way, develop the inner responsible self that takes care of the child's spontaneous self.

"My main point, Professor Kohlberg, is that the child does not have to wait for the highest stage of moral development before he or she is motivated by principles. Motivation by principles happens at the beginning. You missed this crucial point about moral cognition and motivation because you missed the feminine side of your own mind."

This is the kind of response that a keeper of the feminine, one who *cares* about *being,* is likely to give to Kohlberg's overly masculine system.

Kohlberg's masculine emphasis on justice lacks not only an awareness of intuitive cognition, but also a balancing emphasis on love. Justice without love is morally incomplete. So is love without justice. The af-firming kind of love that says, "You are good in your being; do good in your actions," includes justice within itself.

If Kohlberg were more holistic in his starting point, more feminine as well as masculine, his scheme would be more balanced and whole, and women would have no valid reason to react.

Women Still React

A woman's special sense of receptivity is an acutely sensitive, explosive issue today. The masculinized woman does not want to be receptive, much less an affirming keeper of the feminine. She prefers to be a performance-oriented individualist, and a wanting and unwanting, preference-oriented selfist.

Caught in this frame of mind, many feminists react impulsively against the prospect of what seems to them a masculine law that would interfere with their version of responsible choice. Some say that such a law would nationalize their wombs. They do not realize that privatizing their wombs is just as extremely masculine as nationalizing them, and that neither condition is appropriate for *persons.*

A law that cares for human life in all its stages is feminine-masculine, and respects the privacy of everyone, including the privacy of the child in the womb. "Nationalization" is just a terrorizing word that expresses the deeper, pathological fear of women who experience their own bodies as menacing threats.

Responding, not reacting, can dispel this inner terrorism. By receiving her true desire for awareness of her body, for wholeness in her person as a woman, and for integrity in her actions, a reacting woman becomes a responding woman. Her choices, then, are much more likely to be responsible.

CHAPTER FOURTEEN

WHAT WOMEN CAN DO

The time has come for a new women's movement in America. The giant misstep of the previous movement—its forward march into the puritan-playboy trap—cannot be undone by its own ideology and impetus. Many people are ready for a new beginning: another vision and another course of action.

In some ways, the new movement has already begun in the casualties of the old movement. Those women who had abortions, later regretted it, found healing, and now turn around to help their sisters in distress, are beginning to see the new light.

Other women who get involved in the kind of pregnancy counseling that informs women about the consequences of, and alternatives to, abortion, as well as helping them with their needs, readily see that the old movement's abortion-mentality is one of the worst things that can happen to women.

Still other women, along with whole men, are charting a new course in the natural family planning movement.[1] An incipient interest in stewardship of the body is progressing, too, in the emerging fields of natural and holistic health-care. Many women are managers and practitioners in these recently formed health institutions.

Unlike the impetus of the old movement, however, the new one does not dash outward into work, accomplishment, and achievement without first deepening and strengthening the inner source. The new movement has a different philosophy of the

174

working woman, a vision that begins in receptivity and that flowers into expressive action.

The new women's movement is like a potter at the wheel. The more receptive the potter's hands on the clay, the sooner the clay "prepares itself" for shaping. It cannot be formed into a vessel that is both useful and beautiful until centering occurs. Once the clay is centered, the potter can then open it with well-directed hands, and move it into the desired shape.

A beginner at the wheel is inclined to push and pull the clay to get it centered. This kind of performance, even when subtle, is futile. It gets nowhere. The potter must receive the clay as it spins, and hold it firmly, but without manipulation. He or she must wait patiently, and not try to "do" the centering for the clay. If hands are receptive and firm at the same time, the clay finds its own center, and can be shaped, then, with an articulate skillfulness. Inwardly receptive hands become outwardly creative.

The exquisite relation between *receptive centering* and *creative expression* in the art of pottery-making is a significant image for women. We can see this relation, and the need women have for centering within, in two women of the Christian testament: Mary and Martha. Mary received Jesus, their friend, listened to his words, and talked with him. Martha ran off to the workplace and wanted Mary to go with her, apparently to leave their guest alone. Commenting on the situation, Jesus said, "Mary has chosen the better way." He did not mean that Martha's caring work was unimportant, but that it was uncentered in the receiving and contemplating depths of the heart.

There were valiant women in the Hebrew testament. One, however, was more like Martha than Mary. Had she chosen the better way, history would have been a different story. Had Eve been more like Mary, she would have been satisfied to let the tree in the *center* of the garden just be itself. Like Martha, however, she was too concerned about the food-value of the tree, and even felt impelled to use it for her own ulterior purpose. Desiring to become like God in a forbidden way, Eve did not know who she was. That was, and still is, the beginning of the nameless problem.

Centering in the within (in the tree of life), in the presence of the Giver of being, is the better way. Then, as the ancient Chinese philosopher, Lao-tzu, said, "The way to do is to be."

Our stressful puritan culture has no idea what these words might mean. How can we even imagine doing by being? The image of the potter's hands can help us. So can the relationships between Mary, Martha, and Eve.

Another significant image is water. Water does all it does simply by being itself. It nurtures every living thing. All roots reach for it, and all mouths drink it. Water flows under and above the surface of the ground; it evaporates into the air and condenses to renew the earth. Ships move on oceans, sailboats on lakes, swimmers in lakes, rivers, and pools, and little children in the water of their mother's wombs. Flowing water, by receiving whatever stands in its path, simply moves around it and continues on its way.

Water is beautiful. But it can be ugly too. When it overflows its banks, it floods and destroys.

Like the receptive and nurturing power of water, the feminine power within us receives and nurtures life. Keepers of the feminine can accomplish much by *knowing* who they are and by *being* themselves. Women who do not know who they are, and who rush into the workplace to find themselves, are like water that runs over its banks and destroys more than it renews.

Keepers of the feminine, *being* like water, can become especially cognizant of the hidden roots of things. They can "water roots" by affirming others. Affirmed people *spontaneously* grow in their potential.

It is too easy, however, to try to *do* affirmation without first *being* it. The watering done by the affirming heart is not a project, not an achievement. It is simply an act of receiving the gift, letting the heart be warmed by the goodness of the other, and letting the other *feel* this warmth. Then expressive action can be creative and humanly productive.

176

Our puritan-playboy culture cannot teach us this better way. We need to find it first, then bring it into our culture. The American character needs, probably more than anything else, a new women's movement that knows the way of doing by being.

This better way begins when we finally start recognizing our culture for what it is. Woman's nameless problem, is, after all, the nameless problem in the puritan-playboy air we breathe.

Women Can Become Aware

The new women's agenda begins with activities that increase awareness of our culture's character, and of ourselves within this character. Reading and discussing together are valuable pathways to the needed awareness. Women can share their insights as they move toward the images of the new beginning, and away from the playboy images and scripts that dominate our world. They can strengthen each other.

Women can also read, discuss, and share insights with men, moving (after centering) in the direction of a whole-woman, whole-man friendship.

But centering comes first.

As centering women grow in awareness of the puritan-playboy trap in which many are held captive, they do not attack men, as the previous women's movement did. They begin by doing something quite different.

Women Can Forgive

The new women's movement does not begin with reaction and aggression, but with forgiveness. Women verbally attacking men, or trying to prove themselves to men, is an alley that leads into a dark and frustrating corner. Separating themselves from men, or identifying too closely with them, only increases the persisting problem. Women end up empty, sad, and wondering what went wrong.

We need to begin by forgiving the puritan and playboy in the world around us and within us. Understanding who they are, and why they are, helps us to forgive them.

Forgiveness is important because it frees us, in an inner way, from the influences that try to control us. Forgiveness frees us for the centering process.

We *can* forgive men for their domineering tactics. We can also forgive those feminists who have made the feminine mistake and who have led women into the masculine trap. Most importantly of all, we can open our own selves to forgiveness. And we can forgive ourselves for following their lead.

Many women already have submitted themselves to domineering methods of controlling their bodies. A woman might think, for example, "I got my tubes tied and thought it was a good solution to my problem at the time. I didn't stop to ask what I was saying about myself and my sexuality in this final solution. Now I see my solution as another kind of problem. What can I do about it?"

She can increase the awareness she already has. She can forgive those whose cultural scripts encouraged her to make her choice. And she can forgive herself for freely following their lead. Then she can become firm and assertive with the puritan-playboy origins of the domineering mentality and technology that influenced her choice.

This woman might decide to tell others her story, and what she thinks of what she did, and why. If she does not want to do this alone, she can find others who will do it with her. They can study, think, and discuss together. Then they can say it as they see it. They can help others to find a better way.

At the beginning, however, forgiveness can be a long and challenging process of the heart. It is usually not an instant decision. Feelings of deep hurt and anger usually are not healed suddenly. A good friend or a counselor or a minister can help with the process. So can a good book.[2] Prayer is essential.

Forgiveness frees us not only for constructive and creative action, but primarily for the inner deepening of the heart and mind that is the basis, and carrying power, for the new women's movement. The anger and aggression of the previous movement impelled women outward in a premature way. While this outward orientation succeeded in burying the nameless problem, it could not solve the problem. Now we must move within, and only from there into outward action.

From Forgiveness to Inner Deepening

What can women do about the dark and brooding lack of spiritual receptivity in puritanism other than deepening themselves spiritually, and developing in themselves an affirming heart?

I know a woman who has family responsibilities, and who has worked her way up to a managerial position in a local company. She has no more than a high school education. Yet she reads widely and profoundly in psychology, spirituality, and even in the mystics. She is deepening her womanhood whenever she can—in silence, stillness, and contemplation —while longing always for more time to do the same. This woman knows the answer to the nameless problem.

Silence, stillness, and pondering in the heart are receptive. We receive our inner depth. Paradoxically, this deep within is not an enclosure, but an opening into the within of everything else, even the interior life of God. Like an outsider coming in to warm hands at the fire, we enter into God to warm our intuitive hearts and to change our lives.

In her book, *Receiving Woman,* Ann Ulanov says, "Some of us try to discard the notion of God altogether only to find our unlived spiritual drive inflating our political convictions to fantastic proportions. Some of us cast about in a jungle of meditative practices, astrology, health food, jogging. We say we are going inward, but find ourselves instead still in the prison of narcissism."[3] Though political action and health care remain very important for women, only the deepening of spiritual roots is able to lead us and our projects out of the prison of self-fixation.

The spiritual deepening of receptivity that leads us out of puritanism also deepens our sexuality and leads us out of playboyism. Spiritual deepening increases true sexual freedom. Unless the puritan problem is solved, the playboy-playmate problem can only be suppressed, not really solved either.

The feminine power of receptivity liberates the masculine "I can do" and changes the playboy attitude, "I can do nothing about my sexual urges except act them out." The result is "I can receive my sexual feelings and let them become energy for the development of a warm, affirming heart. I can also let my sexual feelings become energy for commitment and for appropriate sexual expression in marriage, including the integration of my generative potential. I am not sexually helpless anymore than I am spiritually helpless."

Women who passively and helplessly accept performance sexuality as an absolute necessity, and the domineering technology that goes along with it, resign themselves to the masculine trap. The original women's movement has not yet begun the liberation that leads to true sexual freedom.

Women can call for a real sexual revolution, and they can do this in their own everyday situations as they find them.

For example, some years ago, one woman began her revolutionary journey when she happened to see her husband driving weavingly down a neighborhood street. Her heart sank as she realized that he was intoxicated. Was he having a problem with alcohol? She later asked him about the incident, and yes, he had been drinking for a long time without letting her know.

Though her husband had a vasectomy, their sex life was unsatisfactory to her. She felt that they lacked emotional intimacy and friendship. An alcohol problem on top of a marriage problem seemed to be more than this woman could bear.

She turned to God in a very intimate and prayerful way, and gradually, with group support and other outside help, stimulated a similar response in her husband. Slowly a sense of sharing developed between them.

One day she wrote a letter to the local newspaper expressing her regret about their choice of a birth control method. She said they would not have made this choice if they had friendship in their marriage at the time.

Gradually the alcohol problem was resolved, and a formerly miserable couple found happiness.

From Inner Deepening to Creative Action

Many women can become promoters of the new awareness in their own families. Others, if they choose, can become secretaries, writers, office workers, teachers, factory workers, physicians, executives, legislators, and more, in ways that reveal the keepers of the feminine.

Women can be hunters, and men can be nurturers. While this might seem like a role reversal, female hunters are not the same as male hunters. Nor are male nurturers the same as female nurturers.

Women can be fatherly, and men can be motherly. But women cannot *be* fathers, nor can men *be* mothers. Any kind of action that is tied to fatherhood, whether by essence or by symbol, might be one that a woman can *do,* but not one that indicates what a woman can *be.*

Because a woman *can do* what a father does, perhaps even better than some fathers, does not mean that she can *be* a father. And her children *know* it, even though they might not be able to explain it, and even though they might be taught how to deny it. The right side of the brain can be overpowered by the left side, but it cannot be destroyed. The right side still *knows*—subconsciously, if not consciously.

Knowing herself as a keeper of the feminine (and of the integration between feminine and masculine), a woman can take action to bring about a new mentality in our culture, and a true sexual revolution. She can do this in her own family, and together with others who share her awareness and interests.

The way for centering and creating in our culture is wide open to us all, men as well as women. But women, with their special emphasis on awareness, wholeness, and sharing, are called to start the new awakening.

Women Can Promote Dominion (Versus Domination) Technology

Women who choose their call to wholeness in a too-masculine world, even if the choice is difficult, are the ones who have real woman power. These women refuse the domination technology that treats their bodies like a defect of nature, and that takes over conception and gestation with lab dishes and artificial wombs. They do not like the womb-envy they see in men who devise technological substitutes for the female role in the generation of life.

Keepers of the feminine can tell men that they do not want a domineering approach to nature, only the kind that receives natural wholeness and serves natural integrity. They can tell puritans and playboys that women's bodies are not diseased, nor are they out of control. These voices of choice can tell men that something else is out of control: the performance-drive in human nature.

Women can demand the reversal of their Constitutional degradation in the whole train of Supreme Court abortion rulings, and they can work to change the abortion culture. They can express their regrets for the puritan-playboy mentality of Margaret Sanger and her organizational progeny, and their domineering, anti-sex approach to the human life-giving power.

182

Keepers of the feminine can make it clear that domination is not the same as dominion. According to *Genesis*, man and woman were given dominion over the earth. But too many of us do not know how to receive this gift.

Dominion begins in affirmation. Domination begins in passivity and helplessness. Dominion is responsible; a domineering attitude is irresponsible. Dominion is careful, cooperative stewardship; it has its origin in "receiving the gift." Domination pushes and pulls without receiving, and without centering.

Women can show how dominion methods of body control are regulation methods that integrate the masculine with the feminine approach to nature, and how domination methods are overly masculine.

Women can expand their care for life beyond control of their own bodies into other dimensions of life and health care; everywhere promoting dominion, versus domination, technology. They can show that too much reliance on drugs and surgeries at the end of the disease process expresses a domineering mentality. Why wait for the disease to progress only to attack its symptoms in the end? The dominion mentality uses natural methods of health care, not drugs and surgeries, to *prevent* the disease-process from starting, or continuing.

Pain, for example, is a symptom that can be killed with drugs. But it is also a warning signal, a "fire alarm," telling us that something is wrong. Drugs often turn off the annoying alarm (blessed relief!) while letting the fire continue to burn.

Waiting to control outward symptoms by removing them is a domination approach to the problem. This kind of control can be necessary, especially if there is no other way to manage distress. Going inward to the cause behind the symptoms, or taking steps to prevent the cause, is a dominion approach. Preventing stress, allergies, and toxic buildup before the disease-process gets started, is much better stewardship than removing cancers and transplanting hearts at the final stage of that same process. Good physical, emotional, and mental nutrition—supplied with a

183

nurturing, not a domineering, attitude toward nature—strengthens the person and prevents dis-ease.

Oriented toward symptoms instead of causes, domination technology is splintered into many separate departments of treatment without any kind of integrating center. Where does this leave the real living person who remains one reality in all of his or her complexity? The need for holistic health-care is critical, and is not being met in the domination culture.

Women can become experts in the holistic, integrated approach to care for human life and well-being, an approach that is mindful of *inner* causes of life, health, and disease. They need not lock themselves into a system of specialties (without an integrating center) that treats the multitude of symptoms.

Many people can tell personal stories about "running all over the country" to various specialists, and finally discovering a combination of specialists that met their needs. No one was there to guide them to this combination. At great loss of time, energy, and money, they had to set out into the wilderness without chart or compass. This absence of the integrating factor leaves a black hole into which women can shine the light of awareness, and take the step of responsible action.

Women Can Make the World a Home

The black hole is there because puritanism and the subsequent Enlightenment saw the world as a mathematical machine. Even animals were called machines. The human body was regarded as a mechanism. It is no wonder that people have come to feel lonely, estranged, and pulled apart in this world.

Who can be fully alive in such a rigidly functional place? Who can feel at home with themselves, or with anyone or anything else, while living in a world that is so mechanized? Who can transform this place into a warm and beautiful home?

The world, of course, has mathematical and mechanical aspects. But trying to turn these mere aspects into basic reality is a kind of crime, the better to dominate the world around us and within us.

The ecological movement is now beginning to warm our sense of the world, and to shine a light on the organic unity of all its systems. At the same time, the ecumenical movement is warming our religious life. Both the ecological and ecumenical movements show a kind of feminine emergence in an overly masculine consciousness. Ironically, at the same time, the original women's movement is strongly reinforcing an overly masculine approach to life.

Women are being called to a new awakening. The earth is rotating on its axis and the sun is appearing, not just outside the window, but within. If we do not see the inner sunrise, if we refuse to receive the warming light, who will? Eve led Adam away from this radiant center within, into coldness, darkness, disintegration, and pain, because she did not know who she was, and did not receive the gift as it was given. Who but the returning Eve, in our power to receive, can lead him back again?

NOTES

Chapter One: Have Women Found Their Way?

1. Betty Friedan, *The Feminine Mystique* (New York: Dell, 1964), p. 16.
2. Anne Wilson Schaef, *Women's Reality* (Minneapolis: Winston, 1981), p. 111.
3. Megan Marshall, *The Cost of Loving: Women and the New Fear of Intimacy* (New York: G. P. Putnam's Sons, 1984, p. 164.
4. Ernest Jones, *The Life and Work of Sigmund Freud* (New York: Basic Books, 1953) Vol. 1, p. 384.
5. The receptive ovum is a symbol of inward being, and the assertive, vigorous, goal-oriented sperm cells are symbols of outward action. Yet both provide *equal* amounts of chromosomes when they unite. While having different orientations, they are, indeed, equal.

Chapter Two: Stepping Into the Masculine Trap

1. For example, see Nona Aguilar, *The New No-Pill, No-Risk Birth Control* (New York: Rawson Associates, 1986).
2. *The Washington Times,* August 3, 1983, Nancyjo Mann interviewed by staff writer and columnist, Tom Diaz. More information about Women Exploited by Abortion is available from W.E.B.A., P.O. Box 267, Schoolcraft, Mich. 49087.
3. *The Uncertified Human*, Toronto, September, 1974.
4. See *The Psychological Aspects of Abortion* edited by David Mall and Walter F. Watts, M.D., (Washington, D.C.: University Publications of America, 1979).

5. Ann Saltenberger's book *Every Woman Has a Right to Know the Dangers of Legal Abortion* (Air-Plus Enterprises, 1982) compiles the evidence from medical journals, medical papers, testimony before Senate subcommittees, World Health Organization documents, and findings of investigative reporters.

6. James C. Neely, M.D., *Gender* (New York: Simon and Shuster, 1981), p. 163.

7. Mall and Watts, op. cit., 50-51.

Chapter Three: **What Women Need to Know About Their Own Minds**

1. Quoted in *Psychiatric Aspects of the Prevention of Nuclear War* (New York: Group for the Advancement of Psychiatry, 1964), p. 223.

2. Jo Durden-Smith and Diane DeSimone, *Sex and the Brain* (New York: Arbor House, 1983), p. 59. This book is a scientific work by investigative writers, and is written in a vivid style that is easy and interesting to read.

3. Neely, op. cit., p. 272.

4. Ibid., p. 273.

5. Durden-Smith and DeSimone, op. cit., p. 205.

6. Ibid., p. 64 and 73.

7. Ibid., p. 73-74. The front part of the left side is verbal, and the back part of this side is wider and projects more. And the visual-spatial part of the right side is in the back part of that lobe, while its front is wider and projects more. Ibid., pages 68, 73, and 166.

8. Ibid., pp. 65-72.

9. Ibid., p. 76. Refers to Christine de Lacoste-Utamsing and Ralph Holloway: "Sexual Dimorphism in the Human Corpus Callosum" (*Science*, June 25, 1982).

10. Carol Gilligan, drawing from Nancy Chodorow (1974), develops this theme in her book, *In A Different Voice*, Harvard University Press, 1982.

11. Durden-Smith and DeSimone, op. cit., p. 73.
12. Ibid., p. 78.

Chapter Four: The Puritan Air We Breathe—
         Overly Masculine

1. Daniel Bell, *The Cultural Contradictions of Capitalism* (New York: Basic Books, Inc., 1976), p. 60-61.
2. Sydney Ahlstrom, *A Religious History of the American People* (New Haven: Yale, 1972), p. 1079.
3. *Puritan Sage,* Collected Writings of Jonathan Edwards, edited by Vergilius Ferm (New York: Library Publishers, 1953), p. 372-73.
4. Perry Miller, *The New England Mind* (New York: Macmillan, 1939), p. 404.
5. Francis J. Bremer, *The Puritan Experiment* (New York: St. Martin's Press, 1976), p. 22.
6. Ibid., p. 23.
7. Miller, op. cit., p. 10.
8. Bremer, op. cit., p. 25.
9. Paul Tournier, *The Gift of Feeling* (Atlanta: John Knox Press, 1981), p. 23.
10. *They Preached Liberty,* edited by Franklin P. Cole (Indianapolis: Liberty Press), p. 18.
11. Ibid., p. 21.
12. Bremer, op. cit., p. 22.
13. Ahlstrom, op. cit., p. 348.
14. Bremer, op. cit., p. 229.
15. Ibid., p. 231. "Calvinism is acknowledged, even by its foes, to have promoted powerfully the cause of civil liberty." (G.P. Fisher, *Reformation,* 1884, p. 239.)
16. For substantiation of the idea in this statement, see Gerhard O. Forde, *Where God Meets Man, Luther's Down-to-Earth Approach to the Gospel* (Minneapolis: Augsburg, 1972).
17. Tournier, op. cit., p. 79.

Chapter Five: Performance Sexuality: From Puritan to Playboy

1. Schaef, op. cit., p. 117-118.
2. Bremer, op. cit., p. 177.
3. Ibid., p. 177.
4. Duncan Crow, *The Victorian Woman* (New York: Stein and Day, 1972), p. 25-26.
5. Bell, op. cit., p. 61-63. This college group included Walter Lippmann, Van Wyck Brooke, John Reed, and Harold Stearns.
6. Ibid., p. 66, p. 224.
7. The affective versus the effective is a theme developed by psychiatrists Conrad W. Baars and Anna Terruwe in *Healing the Unaffirmed* (New York: Alba House, 1976); and Baars, *Born Only Once: The Miracle of Affirmation* (Chicago: Franciscan Herald Press, 1975); and *Feeling and Healing Your Emotions* (Plainfield, N.J.: Logos International, 1979).
8. William Kilpatrick, *Identity and Intimacy* (New York: Dell, 1975), p. 1.
9. This theme of loneliness is developed by David Reisman, *The Lonely Crowd* (New Haven: Yale, 1950).

Chapter Eight: His Impotence Peaks

1. John Locke, *The Second Treatise of Civil Government*.
2. Words of the proclamation: "Inasmuch as the great Father has given us this year an abundant harvest of Indian corn, wheat, beans, squashes, and garden vegetables, and has made the forests to abound with game and the sea with fish and clams, and inasmuch as He has protected us from the ravages of the savages...."
3. John Noonan, *A Private Choice* (New York: The Free Press, 1979), p. 21.
4. Roe v. Wade, Mr. Justice White, p. 2.

5. John Hart Ely, "The Wages of Crying Wolf: A Comment on *Roe v. Wade*," *Yale Law Journal* 82 (1973): p. 920-949.

6. Twinning occurs when the original zygote divides into two or more zygotes. If conception is the beginning of a new person, twinning (tripling, etc.) *appears* to mean that one person divides into others, which is unthinkable. What appears on the surface, however, is not the reality. Conception appears to produce a fertilized ovum. But the result of conception is no longer an ovum at all, nor even a union of sperm and ovum. The result of conception is a new human individual. (On the surface, the sun appears to move around the earth, but, in actuality, does not.)

   Twinning could be a kind of parthenogenesis or natural cloning, in which the original individual survives while begetting (in a single-sex way) another or others. Or twinning could be an event that destroys the first individual—an example of early death—while starting others. In any case, there is no proof whatever that twinning denies the original conception as the beginning of a new person. Even though we do not know until later how many individuals are present, it is unreasonable to suppose that, at conception, there is not *at least one* individual present.

Chapter Nine: Time for a Better Way

1. For a psychology of affirmation, see works of Baars and Terruwe listed in footnote number 7, chapter five above.

2. Alvin Toffler, *The Third Wave* (New York: Bantam Books, 1980), p. 443.

Chapter Ten: How to Live with Our Feelings

1. Paul Warner, M.D., *Feeling Good About Feeling Bad* (Waco, Texas: Word Books, 1979), p. 85.

2. Conrad W. Baars, M.D., *Feeling and Healing Your Emotions* (Plainfield, N.J.: Logos International, 1979), p. 149.

Chapter Eleven: A True Sexual Revolution

1. More on the different kinds of touch appears in the next chapter under the subtitle: "Women Want Sharing."
2. For further reading on human sexuality and man-woman relationships, and for a source referring to numerous relevant readings, see *Human Sexual Ecology* by Robert E. Joyce, Ph.D., University Press of America, 4720 Boston Way, Lanham, MD 20706, 1981.

Chapter Twelve: What Women Really Want

1. Schaef, op. cit., p. 111.
2. Anne Morrow Lindbergh, *War Within and Without* (New York: Harcourt Brace Jovanovich, 1980), p. 230.
3. Tournier, op. cit., p. 100.
4. Daniel Levinson, *The Seasons of a Man's Life* (New York: Alfred A. Knopf, 1978), p. 335.
5. Steven Naifeh and Gregory Smith, *Why Can't Men Open Up?* (New York: Clarkson N. Potter, 1984), p. 30.
6. Ibid., p. 31.
7. In public demonstrations held in New York, Boston, and Minnesota in the fall of 1982, Dutch therapist, Franz Veldman, taught this technique to pregnant women. His *Life Welcomed and Affirmed* (Academie voor Haptonomie en Kinesionomie, Nymegen, Netherlands, 1976) describes his approach to affirming touch.

Chapter Thirteen: Responsible Choice

1. Our responsibility to receive our being (integrative self) is different from our responsibility to receive our feelings and values (responsible self), though the latter emerges within the former. The difference is referred to under the subtitle "Our Integrative Awareness" in Chapter Ten.

2. There are important distinctions in the expression "I am." Saying "I am happy," for example, refers to a changeable state of being. "I am a person" refers to a much more substantial meaning of being that is very close to the basic meaning of existence: "I am." "I am a woman" is substantial too. "I am a mother" is substantial in a different way. Any kind of handicap is a deprivation, and is not substantial. "To be or not to be" refers to our positive substantial nature, and our manhood or womanhood. We can have deprivations in our manhood or womanhood, but these are not the basis on which we receive our being, and choose our actions. Blindness, for example, does not justify lying or stealing.

3. Neither are there two logics, one for women and one for men. The integrative aspect of logic has a feminine emphasis; identity-and-separation has a masculine emphasis. We need the latter emphasis in working out our thinking, but only in the context of a basically integrative endeavor.

4. Carol Gilligan, *In a Different Voice,* Harvard University Press, 1982, p.90.

Chapter Fourteen: What Women Can Do

1. Further information on natural family planning is available ($2.00) from the Human Life Center, Collegeville, MN 56321. The center provides referral to every area of the United States and to some other countries, and publishes the quarterly, *The International Review of Natural Family Planning.*

2. Lewis B. Smedes, *Forgive and Forget* (San Francisco: Harper and Row, 1984).
3. Ann Belford Ulanov, *Receiving Woman* (Philadelphia: The Westminster Press, 1981), p. 150.